OUR CULTURE OF PANDERING

Our Culture of Pandering

PAUL SIMON

Southern Illinois University Press
Carbondale

Printed in the United States of America

06 05 04 4 3 2

Library of Congress Cataloging-in-Publication Data

Simon, Paul, date.
Our culture of pandering / Paul Simon.
p. cm.
Includes bibliographical references and index.
1. Political planning—United States. 2. Political participation—United States. 3. Public opinion—United States. 4. Representative government and representation—United States. 5. Political leadership—United States. 6. Politicians—United States. 7. United States—Politics and government— 2001– I. Title.
JK468.P64.S56 2003
320'.6'0973—dc21 2003005979
ISBN 0-8093-2529-2 (alk. paper)

Printed on recycled paper. ♻

The paper used in this publication meets the minimum requirements of American National Standard for Information Sciences—Permanence of Paper for Printed Library Materials, ANSI Z39.48-1992. ∞

To Patti

Contents

Preface *ix*

1. Pandering in Politics 1

2. Pandering in the Media 59

3. Pandering in Religion 99

4. Pandering in Education 137

Postscript 175

Acknowledgments 181

Notes 183

Index 201

Preface

THIS BOOK is a call to alter our course, to encourage those who hold the titles of leadership to actually lead, and to prod those who are not leaders to demand more of those who hold the titles. After surveying the U.S. political scene, *New York Times* columnist Anthony Lewis concluded, "In public policy, fewer and fewer decisions are made on the substantive merits."[1]

In many ways, our nation has made progress, but the strides forward that we assume are part of our culture did not occur because leaders in the fields of politics, the media, religion, or education did what was popular. Almost all of the big strides forward came because a few leaders defied public opinion. We have lifted the educational level of our people, dramatically improved educational opportunities for young people with disabilities, raised our standard of living (though the lowest one-fifth of our nation's work force has not benefited as much as the rest of us), reduced air and water pollution, extended our lives through health research, and headed the defense of the free world. Yes, we are proud of the advances we have made as a nation and a people, but we are tempted to see only the good, allowing ourselves to take the easy way out, rejecting that which seems difficult, doing and believing what is convenient rather than that which might cause inconvenience.

When I read of a "race riot" in West Frankfort, Illinois, that took place in 1922, it aroused my curiosity because I knew that small coal-mining community had few African Americans. In newspaper files, I discovered that there had been an anti-Italian riot, something unthinkable today. The crude racism of several decades ago, legally mandated in most southern states, is part of history, as is the blatant discrimination that permeated our culture in the northern states. A more sophisticated racism still survives and plagues us, but we have made huge strides forward. Religious tolerance and understanding have generally replaced intolerant zealotry. In the 2000 presidential race, for example, Senator Joseph Lieberman's Jewish roots hardly caused a ripple among the electorate—a far cry from 1960 when the big issue in most parts of the nation was whether we could survive as a democracy if we elected a Roman Catholic president. In part because my father was a member of the Lutheran clergy, as is my brother, I was invited by the 1960 Democratic presidential candidate's brother-in-law, Sargent Shriver, to head the effort to bring balance to this issue in Illinois. But emotions ran high. When I debated this issue in small towns, hundreds of people showed up where ordinarily anyone would have difficulty getting thirty to a political rally. At Wheaton College in Illinois— then more militantly conservative than it is now—I debated an opponent shipped in from Washington, D.C., and it quickly became clear that my wife and my mother were almost alone in being on my side among the one thousand or more who packed the auditorium. Religious prejudice was not new in the United States. In 1903, Utah elected a Mormon to the U.S. Senate, but that body did not permanently seat him for three years, and even then the Senate Judiciary Committee voted seven to five not to seat him. Happily, situations like these seem to be relegated to the past.

We do still face other types of prejudice, however. For instance, prejudice is still present against those whose sexual orientation differs from that of the majority of us, but we now much more openly discuss that issue, which I do not remember being part of our racially sensitive family conversation during my youth. Our willingness to discuss issues of this nature should prevent us from repeating the mistakes of our past.

The aftermath of the criminal tragedy of September 11, 2001, resulted in a few unfortunate anti-Muslim incidents in our country, but from President George W. Bush to grass-roots America, expressions of tolerance were the norm. The occasional lapses from good sense were condemned by a broad spectrum of our society, in contrast to the intolerance we've so often witnessed.

But there is more to the picture. We have spawned "leadership" that does not lead, that panders to our whims rather than telling us the truth, that follows the crowd rather than challenging us, that weakens us rather than strengthening us. It is easy to go downhill, and we are now following that easy path. Pandering is not illegal, but it is immoral. It is doing the convenient when the right course demands inconvenience and courage. Leaders in all areas—including politics, media, religion, and education—are guilty of pandering, of giving in to what is easy instead of fighting for what is right.

In this book, I outline our problems. If we confront those problems and steer toward the more constructive course I advocate—one that requires courage and compassion—people everywhere will benefit.

OUR CULTURE OF PANDERING

1

Pandering in Politics

We are a generation raised on the bizarre proposition that leadership should be equated with popularity. . . . Presidents and prime ministers are not chosen to seek popularity. They are chosen to provide leadership. There are times when voters must be told not what they want to hear but what they have to know. . . . Time is the ally of leaders who place the defense of principle ahead of the pursuit of popularity.

—Brian Mulroney, former Canadian prime minister, in an address at Southern Illinois University, November 1, 2001

"I Am Your Leader, I Am Following You"

We all like to please people. Politicians are not exempt from that trait; when we seek public office or run for reelection, we want to win and usually believe that it is important for the future of a city, county, state, or nation that we succeed. The desire to win has always been part of our political scene, but two things have turned a temptation for candidates into a threat to our free system: First, polls can tell us on a daily basis—hourly, if you want it—what people are thinking. In a zeal to win, political leaders too often use these polls to embrace the whims of public opinion rather than stand firmly for the public interest. Second, campaign contributions now play a huge role in who gets elected. In the process of securing that funding, candidates and, more seriously, officeholders find the time that they should devote to complex issues being devoured by begging for dollars. Equally troubling, those who have the big money have learned that a flow of money to the right candidates pays off handsomely. No stock market purchase will ordinarily reward the investor like this type of investment does. Too often, the winning candidates are those who pander to the polls and to the big campaign contributors.

President Harry S. Truman and Secretary of State George Marshall initiated one of the wisest and most generous acts in the history of the community of nations. Known as the Marshall Plan, it revived the economies of Western Europe and Japan after World War II and saved at least a few of those countries from falling under Communist domination. It has repaid our nation many times over with increased trade and economic activity. Truman and Marshall had humanitarian and policy reasons for their actions, but they also understood the economic lesson of history: When you help others, eventually you help yourself. Six years after the inauguration of the plan, George Marshall received the Nobel Peace Prize, and citizens around the world applauded.

When the United States celebrated the fiftieth anniversary of the Marshall Plan in 1997, we legitimately boasted of the huge contribution the United States made to world stability and opportunity.

But the path to that great national act had serious barriers. A Gallup Poll taken after the announcement of the ambitious plan showed only 14 percent of the American public supporting it. Our leaders asked us to help, among others, the people of Japan, Germany, and Italy who had just killed our men and women in uniform. Truman and Marshall also proposed to help the nations under the military occupation of the Soviet Union, a gesture rejected by the Soviets but also not popular with the American public. European nations that ultimately participated included Austria, Belgium, Denmark, France, Great Britain, Greece, Iceland, Ireland, Italy, Luxembourg, the Netherlands, Norway, Portugal, Sweden, Switzerland, Turkey, and West Germany. All of them experienced substantial growth in their national incomes and then became trading customers with the United States. Everyone benefited dramatically.

However, passage of the Marshall Plan did not come easily, not only because of adverse public opinion but also because President Truman had to deal with a Republican-controlled Congress. Fortunately for our nation and the world, the GOP's Senate foreign policy leader, Senator Arthur Vandenberg of Michigan, made clear that despite the unpopularity of the proposal by the Truman administration, he felt it was in the national interest, and he supported it.

Would an administration of either party today propose something as sweeping as the Marshall Plan without first taking a poll? I doubt it. If a poll came back with such negative numbers, would an administration of either party proceed with the proposal? And ask us to sacrifice for it? I doubt it. If an opposition political party controlled Congress, would that party forego a political advantage to support a proposal by an administration of the other party, even if powerful arguments could be made that it is in the national interest? I doubt it.

The harsh reality is that we have slipped into electing leaders who will not lead, officeholders who are zealous to maintain themselves in power, sometimes at the expense of the national interest. One American historian notes: "As we look over the list of the early leaders of the republic, Washington, John Adams, Hamilton and others, we discern that they were all men who insisted on being themselves. . . . With each succeeding generation, the growing demand of the people that its elective officials shall not lead but merely register the popular will has steadily undermined the independence of those who derive their power from popular election."[1] One political observer reflected, "It is hard to look up to a leader who keeps his ear to the ground."[2] Too often, we have people in legislative and executive offices who act like custodians when we require leadership.

For example, Gail Collins, who covered the 2000 Bush-Gore campaign for the *New York Times*, observed: "The turning point moment for me [in the campaign] would be Elian Gonzalez.* That moment [Gore] came to lose his way, absolutely proved to anybody who might have had a shadow of a doubt, this is a guy who'd do anything to get to be president. . . . There was never a moment in the campaign where I thought I saw a legitimate flash of anger, or even joy, from Al Gore."[3] In fairness, it should be said that Al Gore does feel strongly about some things, in the environmental field particularly. But Gail Collins's criticism is an accurate description of many candidates in both political parties. People want to know, What does the candidate really believe in his or her gut? Does he or she have any convictions? The electorate may be kind to the panderer who mouths what the polls

*Elian is the Cuban boy whose mother fled with him to Florida, but she died on the way. The political controversy revolved around his custody. His father eventually was allowed to take him back to Cuba, a move not popular with many Cuban Americans.

say, but history is kinder to the Harry Trumans, who are genuine leaders.

No matter how kindly voters treat the panderer in the voting booth, the public overwhelmingly believes that candidates will say one thing to get elected and then ignore their pledges once in office. This lack of sincerity, to the extent that happens, reduces public confidence in government. Candidates should say what they believe. At the same time, the public should demand that candidates speak frankly and truthfully about issues of concern, and it must understand that once a person is elected and looks at the facts in much greater detail, changes in attitude do and should occur.

Perhaps more than anything else, the public must educate itself, not just about politics and political candidates but about local, national, and international issues; people must become involved. This is something most of us have not done. In one of the most fascinating and provocative books of recent years, *Bowling Alone*, written by Robert Putnam, the author writes: "As recently as 1960, only 41 percent of American adults had graduated from high school; in 1998, 82 percent had. In 1960 only 8 percent of American adults had a college degree; in 1998, 24 percent had. Between 1972 and 1998 the proportion of all adults with fewer than twelve years of education was cut in half, falling from 40 percent to 18 percent. . . . The growth in education should have increased civic engagement."[4]

Why didn't it? Television has mesmerized us and gobbled up huge chunks of our time. That's a partial answer. Watching television is seldom a social activity. We don't exercise socially or physically while watching the set. When I observe my grandchildren watching television, I notice that they ordinarily say not a word to each other. That may be less true of adults, but genuine conversation about anything rarely takes place as adults watch television. Computers and the Internet add another complicated layer to this. We are not only bowling alone but are much more frequently living alone and driving to work alone rather than carpooling. We're not discussing with others what's happening in the world around us. Part of the problem is that candidates too often sound alike. "It doesn't make any difference how or whether I vote" is a refrain I have heard often, but that deceptively attractive bit of misinformation existed long before our education level went up and our participation declined. "They're all the same. The candidates don't stand for anything" is another refrain, sometimes accurate, sometimes not. I heard it frequently when Hubert Humphrey opposed Richard Nixon, and there were huge differences between them. But to the extent that candidates simply follow the polls, they *will* sound alike, because the polls are telling both sides the same thing.

Columnist Walter Shapiro concludes that "the most vulnerable aspect of the Clinton record may be the president's well-deserved reputation as a poll-propelled weathervane."[5] In fairness, there were areas where President Clinton stood up to both polls and major contributors. On the student loan issue, he took pressure from the banks and did not waver; he had a commitment to racial justice that may have helped him in the North but hurt him in the South. He solidly supported moves toward greater free trade, a stand that did not please his labor union supporters. However, too often survey results overcame his fundamentally good instincts. The *Times* of London commented, "As the dreadful Clinton experience has shown, improvisation without a governing philosophy to hold it in check can easily degenerate into a shiftless, poll-driven opportunism."[6] Taking a poll to determine where to go on vacation, as Dick Morris did for Clinton, is silly but not harmful, but having him survey whether or not to tell the truth about Monica Lewinsky displayed a moral gap. If, at that point, President Clinton had simply stated that he had made a serious mistake and apologized to his family and the nation, there would have been no impeachment vote in the House. In a telling comment about too many pollsters and officeholders, journalist Elizabeth Drew wrote that Dick Morris apparently did not understand "that politics should be for the purposes of governing—that governing shouldn't be for the purpose of politics."[7] There is also the simple reality that complex policy-making decisions cannot accurately be described in a one-sentence polling question.

Even basic religious documents have admonitions of "not following the crowd." According to the Gospel of Luke, Jesus said, "Woe to you when all men speak well of you, for that is how their fathers treated the false prophets."[8] A political leader who tries too hard to please and does what is popular is indeed a false prophet.

Almost two thousand years ago, Plutarch wrote:

> For this is indeed the true condition of men in public life, who, to gain the vain title of being the people's leaders and governors, are content to make themselves the slaves and followers of all the people's humours and caprices. . . . These men . . . steered by popular applause, though they bear the name of governors, are in reality the mere underlings of the multitude. . . . As Phocion answered King Antipater, who sought his approbation of some unworthy action, "I cannot be your flatterer and your friend," so these men should answer the people, "I cannot govern and obey you."[9]

If this concerned Plutarch centuries ago, doesn't this suggest that nothing has changed? What has changed dramatically is the means of communication and the ability to take scientific measurements of public opinion. One of the more thoughtful officials in the nation in recent decades, former New York governor Mario Cuomo, writes: "Poll-watching politicians respond with Pavlovian sureness. They touch every button, satisfy every rabid craving with swift passage of draconian and regressive measures. They serve up a binge of new death penalty statutes as though they had suddenly discovered proof that the death penalty saves lives."[10]

He added that the victims of this rush to massive penalties are "the immigrant, the prisoner, the poor, children, people who can't vote or won't vote. Offered up to assuage the discomfort and anger of an unhappy majority." Despite the costs to others in trying to obey the polls, political leaders, like the rest of humanity, prefer the sound of applause to harsh criticism; they prefer to be reelected rather than defeated. Today a 30-second negative commercial can be produced quickly, with widespread distribution, and office-holding or office-seeking men and women sometimes shake in fear at the prospect of facing that distorted criticism. Too often, there is less fear of hurting others than of being hurt.

While the polling techniques of today are a new political phenomenon, some following of public opinion always takes place in a nation that freely elects its leaders. Candidates who veer too far from public opinion are not likely to be elected. All of us who hold or have held public office will admit—if we are honest—that sometimes we follow the public on matters we believe are of limited importance. For example, in my younger years as a state legislator, I paid little attention to changes in the law affecting wills and estates. On these matters, my votes usually combined the expressions of public opinion in my mail, together with the advice of those in the state legislature who had more knowledge in these matters. The full legislative agenda is not one any single member can totally master. We tend to pay attention to the issues that interest us greatly, or interest the public, or are part of our committee assignments. Did I cast some bad votes on matters relating to wills and estates? I probably did.

Legislators and executives—and even the courts—have never been totally free from either polls or campaign contributions. But the needle in our democracy machine that gauges our dependence on these things has shifted from moderately dangerous to perilous, particularly in the legislative and executive branches. Let's look at a few examples.

Foreign Policy

Foreign policy is particularly subject to the temptation to follow public attitudes rather than to lead. Former Secretary of State Henry Kissinger concludes his most recent book stating that the world "desperately needs enlightened leadership."[11] At least for the immediate years ahead, that must come from the United States. However, most of our recent presidents came into their responsibilities ill-prepared for the international duties of that office, the senior George Bush being an exception. Each improved in understanding the international situation as he served, but frequently, much of the first two years in office were awkward. Presidential election campaigns give little attention to foreign policy, reflecting the disinterest of the American public. Our less-than-primitive understanding of the rest of the world causes us to elect too many leaders who mirror our disinterest and lack of knowledge. When I take a taxi in a large city, the driver is frequently and obviously not an American by birth. When I ask where he or she is from, the reply is frequently "West Africa" or some vague regional designation, assuming correctly that most Americans would ordinarily not have any idea of the nation if it were named. Most of us have no concept of the immensity of the Sudan or Algeria, or that Algiers is closer to London than to Tindouf in Algeria; that St. Petersburg in Russia is closer to New York City than to Vladivostok, also in Russia, or that Vladivostok is closer to Seattle than to Moscow. Most of us are not aware that the United States sells more to Chile, with its fourteen million people, than to India, with its more than one billion, or that we sell almost as much to tiny Costa Rica as to all of eastern Europe. Canada's former prime minister Brian Mulroney, a leader on trade matters, predicts that by the year 2010 the United States "will be exporting more to Latin America than to Europe and Japan combined."[12]

This unhappy combination of a disinterested and poorly informed public and ill-prepared leadership is compounded when policy decisions are made by polling. Kissinger accurately notes, "American foreign policy [has become] increasingly driven by domestic politics."[13] That is a danger in any government. The tensions between India and Pakistan are caused in part by the desire of each leader to please his domestic audience. But when the dominant power in the world has inadequately informed leadership that panders to domestic polls to make foreign policy decisions, the trust in, and effectiveness of, that leadership is weakened.

Consider Somalia and foreign aid. We went into Somalia—a Muslim nation, it should be noted—to rescue a people with virtually no government, to prevent more massive starvation. Somalia had no oil or other natural resources that interested us. To his great credit, the senior George Bush made a decision to intervene in Somalia, and that action saved literally hundreds of thousands of lives. It is one of the few examples in the history of nations where a major world power deployed a sizable number of troops purely for humanitarian purposes. We had no short-term economic, political, or military benefit—only the saving of lives. But during the process, a retired U.S. admiral, working for the United Nations, made a decision relating to a Somali warlord without consulting with the marine general in charge of American troops, Anthony Zinni, and without consulting U.S. ambassador Robert Oakley. The admiral's poorly informed decision, made in good faith, cost the lives of eighteen U.S. armed forces personnel, one of whom was dragged through the streets and shown on television around the world. Immediately, many members of Congress clamored to get our troops out of Somalia. I warned that such a decision would send a signal to terrorists around the world that all they need to do, if American troops are involved, is to kill a few Americans, and we would leave. A lengthy meeting with the new president at the White House resulted in a compromise: Our troops would stay until March and then be withdrawn. President Clinton, presiding at the White House meeting, said little; I sensed that he was uncomfortable dealing with an issue on which he had limited background. Secretary of State Warren Christopher, amazingly, said nothing throughout the lengthy meeting. What we had not made clear to the American public was that leadership requires sacrifice, that building a world of peace and opportunity and justice sometimes requires that we suffer casualties, much as we try to avoid them, that we cannot move into Somalia or Kosovo or Afghanistan briefly and then pull out, leaving an unstable situation. Interestingly, in an ABC television interview given before the tragedies of September 11, 2001, Osama bin Laden gave as one of the reasons for his willingness to attack the United States that we are "a paper tiger," that when we lost eighteen armed service personnel in Somalia, we ran. The Somalia decision came less than two decades after our exit from Vietnam, an unhappy experience seared in our minds. We went from experiencing 58,000 needless casualties in that conflict almost to the point of being unwilling to accept any necessary casualties.

The ease with which we seemingly forget and dismiss the troubles of others has not endeared us to other nations. A survey of foreign leaders by the *International Herald Tribune* three months after the September 11 attack found less support for the United States than had been anticipated. One criticism that leaders voiced: The world's wealthiest nation has not paid much attention in recent years to the world's poor, permitting the gap between the world's wealthiest and poorest to grow. That probably startled many Americans. Most of our citizens inaccurately believe that we are doing more than any other nation in helping the world's poor, and for several years—under the Marshall Plan—we did. Today, both in absolute dollars and as a percentage of our gross national income, it is not true. When those in almost any audience suggest that we should cut out "so much foreign aid" and devote our money to problems at home, I ask what percentage of our budget they think goes for foreign aid. They usually guess 15 to 25 percent. In reality, less than one-half of 1 percent of our budget goes for foreign economic aid. Of that amount, about one-third goes to Israel and Egypt to maintain stability in that region, which is important to us, and the balance to the other nations of need. Of the twenty-two wealthiest nations, our percentage of national income (gross domestic product) that goes for this cause is dead last. Denmark, the Netherlands, and Norway each contribute at least seven times more than we do on a percentage basis. Relative to all the other wealthy nations, we contribute less than half of what they average as a percentage of income. On top of that, because of our huge debt burden, caused primarily by imprudent fiscal management in the 1980s, more than 26 percent of that debt is held outside of our country by banks and wealthy people. As a result, we spend *at least* four times as much through interest payments in what could accurately be termed "foreign aid to the wealthy" than we do for foreign aid for the poor. President Ronald Reagan suggested—but did not follow through—that we should devote 1 percent of our national income (not the federal government's budget) to assist the world's most miserable. Where are we now? At only one-tenth of 1 percent. We perceive ourselves as being generous, but the reality is that in aid to the world's poor we are behind countries like Spain and Portugal.

Five billion of the earth's six billion people receive 20 percent of the world's income. And because of the growing education gap between the industrial nations and the developing world, the income gap is also growing, and that does not help world stability nor discourage terrorism. People with nothing to risk sometimes take irrational actions. A Nigerian writer notes, "With the changing political climate around the world, economics plays a much larger role than weapons of war in influencing world events."[14]

The United States leads the world in defense expenditures and in the sale of arms to other countries, but the battle in which we are engaged today is for the hearts and minds of the developing nations. While we lag behind all other industrial nations in helping the world's poor, with the adoption of the fiscal year 2003 budget for defense we are spending more in that field than the next twenty-six nations combined. What may be effective in destroying a building is not necessarily effective in winning hearts and minds. We need weapons to assist in maintaining a stable world, but weapons alone will not do it. The people of the world look for leadership they can trust, that is stable, that is compassionate, that is interested in their plight. Pious speeches alone can even be counterproductive. We are understandably judged by our actions more than by our words.

In an unusually blunt assessment, UN Secretary-General Kofi Annan told University of Notre Dame graduates, "It is particularly shameful that the United States, the most prosperous and successful country in the history of the world, should be one of the least generous in terms of the share of its gross national product it devotes to helping the world's poor."[15] Mahatma Gandhi spoke accurately a half-century ago: "The earth provides enough to satisfy every man's needs, but not every man's greed."[16] If we were more responsive, it is highly unlikely that—prior to September 11, 2001—the UN Economic and Social Council would have voted to remove the United States from the Commission on Human Rights in a secret ballot. As an additional message to us, it seated the Sudan and Libya, two nations with dismal records in this field.

In an unusual statement by some of this nation's top retired diplomatic and military leaders, they stated:

> There is a general consensus on the need to adequately fund our defenses, [but] there remains widespread indifference about our investment in foreign affairs spending. At the time the National Security Act was passed in 1947, our

> defense spending was only double that of foreign affairs spending, a 2:1 ratio. Throughout the Cold War that ratio was 15:1. Now, a decade after the Cold War, the ratio is still 15:1. . . . Our diplomacy, support for international institutions *and* foreign aid have not received the investment [they should receive].[17]

The report also notes a great flaw: "We need to restrain our own arrogance." Too often, in State of the Union addresses, presidents boast about our being the greatest nation on the face of the earth. Let others say that about us, if they wish, but even if it "plays well in Peoria," it does not in the rest of the world. Secretary of State Madeleine Albright succumbed to that temptation: "If we have to use force, it is because we are America; we are the indispensable nation. We stand tall. We see further than other countries into the future."[18] That's great talk for a domestic audience but not for the other 96 percent of the world. *Chicago Tribune* columnist Steve Chapman touched on a related problem: "We often resemble one of those talking dolls that has an inexhaustible voice but no capacity for hearing."[19]

We owe it to others to listen, to hear, and to help, whether in the form of education to feed the hungry mind or grain to feed the hungry belly. The problems are many. For instance, since the tragic events of September 11, more attention has been paid to the Muslim schools in Pakistan run by extremists who give children who otherwise could not attend school their only chance for an education, but it is not one in the traditional "reading, writing, and arithmetic"; instead, it is in religious zealotry. A year after stepping down as president, Bill Clinton wrote: "A year's education adds 10 percent to 20 percent to a person's income in a poor country. There are 100 million children who never go to school—half of them in sub-Sahara Africa. In Pakistan the main reason that all those madrasses [Muslim extremist schools] were not teaching math but promoting such ludicrous notions as

'America and Israel brought dinosaurs back to Earth to kill the Muslims' is that the Pakistanis ran out of money in the 1980s to support their schools."[20] We could have helped.

Speaking one month after the September 11 attack, ninety-six-year-old former Nebraska governor Frank Morrison noted: "Abraham Lincoln once said this nation cannot exist half-slave and half-free. The world cannot exist 25 percent overfed and 75 percent underfed."[21] We could do more to fight for the freedom of those who are not free, and we could help feed more of the world's hungry.

John F. Kennedy had one of the three shortest inauguration speeches in our presidential history. Listen to these ringing words he spoke a few minutes after having taken the oath of office:

> To those people in the huts and villages of half the globe struggling to break the bonds of mass misery, we pledge our best efforts to help them help themselves, for whatever period is required—not because the communists may be doing it, not because we seek their votes, but because it is right. If a free society cannot help the many who are poor, it cannot save the few who are rich.[22]

An Oxford University scholar writes: "In the 1960's, the richest fifth of the world's population had a total income 30 times as great as the poorest fifth's; in 1998, the ratio was 74:1. In 1965, real gross domestic product per capita in Chad was one-fifteenth of the U.S.'s; in 1990, one fiftieth. . . . Such inequality seems likely to increase the resentment in poorer countries toward the super-rich United States."[23] What is our sacrifice today for the world's poor? About twelve cents per day for each citizen through our government and one-half cent per day through various charities. What happened to Kennedy's stirring vision?

If we were more responsive, the bin Ladens of the world would have a harder time portraying us as ogres. Why are we not more responsive? In part, the polls. When listing areas that should be cut in a federal budget—education, health, agriculture, and foreign aid, among others—people pick foreign aid as the place where they would apply the scissors. But ask the question differently: Should we help hungry people in Ethiopia or Afghanistan? Then the public responds overwhelmingly favorably. Such action requires a little courage on the part of presidents and members of the House and Senate. In any election or reelection campaign, a supporter of foreign aid is likely to be on the defensive initially, but it can quickly be turned around, and by the end of the campaign the opponent is likely to be mute on this issue.

Leon Aron of the American Enterprise Institute writes:

> Poor democracies are now more numerous than regimes of any other type. . . . Many Western experts and journalists have forgotten that democracy is not an all-or-nothing affair, but a system toward which a political culture may advance in fits and starts . . . by minute but cumulatively momentous steps. . . . The progress of the poor democracies in the coming years is our best hope of diminishing poverty and violence in the world. . . . The poor democracies . . . deserve aid and encouragement, not neglect and disdain.[24]

Unfortunately, there are too many examples of his point. Liberia, a nation in Africa founded by former American slaves, has more historic ties to the United States than any other African country, yet we paid little attention to it as long as the leadership sided with us in the cold war with the Soviets. We ignored the abuses. In 1997, they finally had a nationwide free election, former president Jimmy Carter and I cochairing the international team monitoring it. Unfortunately, the person elected, Charles Taylor, has pursued his personal financial agenda rather than the national interest, and today the capital city, Monrovia, still does not have such basics as a water system or electricity, and the national unemployment rate is a staggering 85 percent. Earlier and consistent interest on our part could have helped develop a very different life for that nation and region.

Next to Liberia is Sierra Leone, a nation with difficulties generated in part from neighboring Liberia. When Sierra Leone experienced the beginnings of a civil war motivated by financial interests, UN Secretary-General Kofi Annan appealed to the United States, among other nations, to respond. The *New York Times* reported: "Mr. Annan would like to send in sophisticated and experienced military teams to assess problems or set up missions. But the United States prefers to see missions in Sierra Leone carried out by other countries, many of them poorly equipped, lesser trained troops."[25] He then asked us to airlift troops into the country. We said we would do it for $17 million to $21 million. Instead, the United Nations chartered a commercial airline for $6 million.

In another example, Mike Moore, director general of the World Trade Organization, told an international gathering in Monterey, Mexico, that "the agricultural subsidies paid out by the United States and the European Union cost the developing nations more than $250 billion a year in lost markets—more than five times the sum of all the aid they receive."[26]

During my House service, I made a speech in behalf of foreign aid. One of my House colleagues, Representative Richard Kelly of Florida, said he completely agreed with me, that providing foreign aid helped the goals of our nation. Then he added, "I only wish I could vote with you." I asked why he couldn't, and he responded that the people in his district opposed it. "How do you know that?" I asked. He said that his mail showed it. How many letters had he received in the last month against foreign aid? "Probably half a dozen," he replied. Six people had frightened him into voting against something he believed to be in the national interest. Later, FBI agents caught him on film in the Abscam scandal, shoving money into his pockets. He served time in prison for that. Legally, the latter action differed from the foreign aid vote. But morally, which was worse, voting against food for hungry people or accepting a bribe?

One thoughtful observer notes: "Pandering's first cousin is demagoguery, and you get a lot of it with the foreign aid question. Not only have public officials failed to stand up to the challenge of our international commitments, but they have intentionally distorted the truth, playing on Americans' natural isolationist tendencies."[27] Complicating things further, our system of financing campaigns means that contributions will reach policy makers for votes favorable to defense, for tax cuts, for farm subsidies—and many other things—but voting aid for sub-Sahara Africa helps not at all. Spinelessly following public sentiment or campaign contributions is a serious affliction in our body politic.

Civil Liberties

In almost every national emergency, there are well-intentioned leaders who want to forget constitutional niceties and "attack the problem," whatever the problem is. Usually those attacks, whether constitutional or unconstitutional, have been popular. In February 1942, President Franklin D. Roosevelt ordered 115,000 Japanese Americans to sell everything they owned in three days and to pack what they wanted into one suitcase because they were to be taken off to camps. His action achieved huge popularity, and even the Supreme Court in the *Korematsu* decision knuckled under to public opinion and approved the president's action. Not one of those 115,000 people was ever accused of committing a crime. We look back on it now with national embarrassment. We have formally apologized as a nation and paid symbolic reparations to those interned in the camps, but we haven't learned our lesson.

After the terrorist activities of September 11, Attorney General John Ashcroft took some actions of—at best—questionable constitutionality and even talked about military tribunals in which people could be tried in secret, with no choice as to a lawyer, no access to evidence, and no appeal to a civilian court. The top penalty: execution. The attorney general justified these proposals by saying, "A gang of cut-throat aliens are a menace to our nation. . . . Detention does not constitute imprisonment, nor even deprivation of liberty without due process of law."[28] What is it then? As of this writing, hundreds of people are still being detained and held incommunicado, and in many instances not even the names have been released. Do we want to stop the terrorists? Of course. Should we have to give up basic civil liberties? No.

This heading on a story is one of many that could be used to illustrate the point: "U.S. Argues War Detainee Shouldn't See a Lawyer."[29] It is about an American citizen being held for several months in Virginia after being captured in Afghanistan. The next day's newspaper had an Associated Press story about the Justice Department's authorization to the FBI to more closely monitor American citizens because of the September 11 tragedy, even if no crime is suspected. The chairman of the House Judiciary Committee, Congressman James Sensenbrenner, Republican of Wisconsin, to his credit is quoted as saying, "I believe the Justice Department has gone too far."[30] William Safire, a former speech writer for Richard Nixon and a conservative columnist for the *New York Times*, noted the abandonment of the requirement for some "reasonable indication of criminal activity" before there is a federal inquiry into any citizen. "*With not a scintilla of evidence of a crime being committed* the feds will be able to run full investigations for one year. . . . This is not some nightmare of what may happen some day. It happened last week" (Safire's emphasis).[31]

There have been too many stories like this *Washington Post* item: "A former Boston cab driver once identified by authorities as a major terrorism suspect was kept in solitary confinement for more than eight months here [in New York City] without seeing a judge or being assigned a lawyer."[32] It turns out there was apparently no basis for the allegation. Treating him that way—

even if the allegation were true—simply should not happen in the United States. In a dictatorship, we might expect that, but not in a free country.

Another popular but wrong move is a Justice Department effort "requiring tens of thousands of Muslim and Middle Eastern visa holders [in the United States] to register with the government and be fingerprinted" and fingerprinting Muslims and people from "sensitive nations" when they enter the United States.[33] We should not make special laws or regulations for people of one religion or of one national background. If the government wants to fingerprint everyone who comes into the nation, that would be constitutional, although probably unwise. But the planned policy, which blatantly discriminates, is offensive to many outside our border whom we need in the struggle with terrorism and is clearly contrary to the spirit of our Constitution.

Part of this Justice Department zealotry is a natural but unwise reflex action to September 11, but part may be an effort to signal "we're really paying attention to this problem" in response to earlier missteps. On September 9—two days before the attack of September 11—Secretary of Defense Donald Rumsfeld threatened a presidential veto if Congress moved $600 million out of the controversial missile shield program into counterterrorism. On September 10—one day before the tragedy—Attorney General Ashcroft submitted the Justice Department budget that asked for increases in sixty-eight programs but "none of them directly related to combating terrorism."[34]

We've faced this zealotry before. During the McCarthy era, for example, the University of Chicago came under great pressure because it had faculty members who took the position that they should not have to swear that they were not Communists, that political freedom meant exactly that. Compounding this problem, the university had two courses that taught about Communism. When probers asked the feisty president of the university, Robert Hutchins, if Communism was still being taught in political science, he responded, "Yes, and cancer at the medical school."[35]

Freedoms are easier to give away than to protect. The applause of the crowd should not stop legislators and other leaders from speaking out in behalf of our civil liberties. One historian talks about "the permanent spirit of inquisition" that haunts us during times of national emergency.[36] During times like these, there is an understandable rallying around a nation's leader. That can be good, but it carries with it the danger that, in the let's-pull-together mood, basic freedoms will be eroded. Almost always, the erosion of those liberties is temporarily popular.

Social Security

One of the most significant policy areas we have to deal with, having long-term consequences for our economy, is the financing of the Social Security Retirement Trust Fund. Not only has Social Security become an important source of income for retirees and their dependents but it has dramatically reduced poverty in the senior age group from 35 percent to less than 10 percent—and gives the economy a solid, steady source of revenue and economic stimulus. But we are headed for trouble.

During the first years of Social Security payments, we had 16 people working for each retiree. That is now down to 3 for each retiree, and it eventually will be 2.3 for each retiree. You do not have to be an economic Einstein to understand that spells trouble. In 2002, we are still paying into the Social Security Retirement Fund more than we are dispensing in benefits, but that will change. By 2016, Social Security will pay out more than it takes in, and by 2038, it is projected to go broke.

The difficulty with facing this problem is that *real* answers are unpopular. One "solution" is to permit people to invest some of their own money, a solution the stockbrokers love. This is based on the assumption that the stock market will generate more wealth than government bonds. The performance of the stock market in the years 2000 to 2003 should shake some confidence in that proposal. It also ignores the reality that during the period December 31, 1964, to December 31, 1981—seventeen years—the Dow Jones average grew by less than one point. And the inflation rate of 103 percent for the same time span makes that figure even worse. Government bonds look great, compared to that. Nor does this proposal for private investment consider the almost unbelievable task and cost of auditing these millions of accounts. One former high administration official said that the risk factor for seniors could be eliminated if the federal government guaranteed the investments. I would love to have someone guarantee my investments! But it is hardly sound government policy to do so. The savings and loan disaster cost the federal government more than $657 billion, including interest, but that expenditure would look small indeed compared to this one. To counter the simplistic appeal this proposal has, some Democrats have suggested that a special board invest about one-third of the Social Security retirement dollars in selected stocks. The board, it is alleged, would be nonpolitical. I've heard that before! Even if that were possible, would we really want the federal government to become the largest stockholder in General Motors and hundreds of other U.S. corporations?

President Bill Clinton had two forums on Social Security retirement, giving people the chance to express their views. He said only two things were not on the table: increased taxes or reductions in benefits. The Speaker of the House, Republican Dennis Hastert, has taken the same stand. The reality is that there are only two ways of solving the problem: some combination of a slight increase in taxes and a slowing of the growth in benefits. A reporter for the *New York Times* observed, "Most politicians have steered clear of supporting higher taxes or lower benefits."[37]

Four of us who are former senators—two Republicans (Alan Simpson of Wyoming and John Danforth of Missouri) and two Democrats (David Pryor of Arkansas and the author)—hoping to get this issue off dead center, proposed covering all income by Social Security, not just the first $80,400. For the person making $1 million a year, that would cost him or her $56,000—not a bad price to pay for the economic well-being of that person's grandchildren. We recommended correcting the consumer price index, which would slow the growth of Social Security payments. The actuary for Social Security said that these relatively modest changes would protect the system for seventy-five years, barring any major economic disaster. However, legislators are not jumping at the opportunity to vote on these sensible but unpopular changes.

If *in addition* to protecting Social Security, the twin goals of increased investment and increased income for seniors are desired, the federal government could modify a suggestion of the Clinton administration and of George W. Bush's Social Security Commission. They suggest that $40 billion be used to match 1 percent of the first dollars of a worker's income for investment purposes. For example, if 1 percent of the first $20,000 made by anyone earning $50,000 a year or less were matched by the federal government, that would make up to $400 a year that could be invested or put into a savings account. It could not be withdrawn—or the stocks sold for cash—until the worker reached the age of sixty-two, although the assets could be passed to his or her heirs if the person died before that time. It would enrich retirement years. It would encourage investment without jeopardizing Social Security retirement funds. It also would slightly reduce the growing gap between the more fortunate and the less fortunate in our nation. By modifying the formula, something less than $40 billion could be spent by the federal government.

Anyone who studies the problem seriously knows that we

should face reality. Why do both political parties duck it? The *St. Louis Post-Dispatch* editorialized on the Social Security problem and concluded, "America can cower under the covers for 15 more years until the monster pops out. . . . Or we can demand leaders who aren't afraid of taking on monsters."[38]

Taxes

The Social Security dilemma for lawmakers includes the hot-button item of taxes. The public image—fostered by irresponsible political speeches—is that we are overtaxed. When compared with western Europe and Japan (when their industrial compact is included), we have a lower total tax burden—federal, state, and local—as a percentage of income than any of these nations, with the possible exception of Turkey.

When we had huge deficits, British prime minister Margaret Thatcher asked a few of us in the Senate visiting her, "Why don't you raise taxes and get rid of the deficit?" In the parliamentary system, that is fairly simple, but not in ours. To the credit of the British, their economic system turned around when they exercised fiscal discipline, including raising taxes. The Reagan tax cut, which we were told would balance the budget in three years, instead headed us toward record-breaking deficits —larger deficits under Ronald Reagan than from all previous presidents from George Washington through Jimmy Carter combined. Fortunately, the senior George Bush and Bill Clinton—one a Republican and one a Democrat—saw that the deficits spelled huge, long-range troubles for the nation, so they asked for and got—barely—tax increases that sent interest rates down and the economy sailing smoothly for the longest period in our nation's history. Because of what he felt was politically popular, Bush told the GOP convention in 1988 when he first ran for election: "Read my lips. No new taxes." But he felt compelled, in the national interest, to eat his words. Bill Clinton in 1993 asked for a tax increase and passed it in the House with no votes to spare—though he felt politically obliged later to say he regretted asking for it. Both deserve credit for the revived economy.

It took massive arm-twisting by both presidents to achieve this laudable goal. Why? Because the polls said people don't want increased taxes, and it was too complicated for weak-kneed legislators to explain that the nation would benefit. If you ask people whether they want a tax cut, poll numbers show strong approval. But ask, Do you want to borrow money from your children and grandchildren so that you can have a tax cut? and you will get a totally different response.

Part of our deficit has come from government waste, something that the public understandably wants to get rid of. But the greatest waste, far outnumbering all other senseless spending combined, is the payment of interest on the national debt. This massive interest expenditure could be avoided if candidates and officeholders stopped pandering to the public by providing tax cuts even when we are running deficits. How big is this problem? The gross interest expenditure by the federal government for fiscal year 2002 will be approximately $330 billion, and for FY 2003, the estimate is $336 billion. By comparison, in FY 1962, the federal government for the first time had a total budget for everything that topped $100 billion. Foreign central bank holdings of U.S. government bonds, or their records of ownership by citizens in their countries, in September 2002 totaled $805 billion. However, because many nations forbid their citizens to hold bonds of other countries, the actual total held by people outside the United States is appreciably larger. Many keep the bonds in a U.S. or Swiss bank—or in some other country—drawing the interest regularly. Even if the total were only the $805 billion and no additional hidden amount existed, at 4 percent interest that would be more than $30 billion, while our total developmental assistance for the poor of other countries is less than $10 billion. The real figure of bonds held outside the United States is substantially greater than $805 billion. In effect, our largest foreign aid expenditure is in the form of interest payments to the wealthy.

By competing in the private domestic market for borrowing, the federal government also sends interest rates up, a hidden tax on people who borrow to buy a car or a home. Higher interest rates also discourage long-term investment that would add to the nation's productivity. Unfortunately, to many officeholders, the problem of deficits is "small potatoes" compared to the votes they can get by promising people tax cuts or increases in spending without additional revenue. In a choice between fiscal prudence and getting votes, fiscal prudence loses out.

The Reagan tax cut of 1981 hurt the nation. Sadly, in response to the public clamor, the Democratic alternative that year was almost as bad. Pandering became a substitute for leadership. Frequently cited as a political reason for caving in to this biennial siren call for tax cuts is the Walter Mondale experience in 1984, when he told the Democratic convention that in response to the huge deficits, taxes would have to be raised. Timid Democratic leaders blanched, and pressure became so great that Mondale reversed his position. But it should be noted that the high point in the public opinion polls for Mondale was immediately after he told the American people the truth.

Crime

Listen to candidates for office, and at some point there is likely to be an easy applause line: They are *really* going to be tough on crime! A few in the audience may not join in the paroxysm of applause, but most will. Few candidates suggest that, yes, we should be tough on crime, but we should also be smart on crime. Where has this clamor to be "tough on crime" led us?

We have a higher percentage of people in our prisons and jails than any other nation—and we have one of the highest crime rates. For the year 2000, we had 702 inmates per 100,000 population in our prisons and jails. Russia was second, with 675, Canada had 115, Mexico 110. Two governments in Africa that are showing the way to stable democracies, Mali and Ghana, each imprisons 30 per 100,000, and Mali has severe poverty and an average life span of only forty-six years. Only one-third of all nations have incarceration rates above 150—which is less than one-fourth of our rate—and almost all of those with rates above 150 still have much lower rates than ours. With 4 percent of the world's population, we have 25 percent of the world's prisoners.[39] Former Secretary of State Henry Kissinger notes three things Europeans know about our nation's policies: the inadequacy of our health insurance coverage, our use of the death penalty, and the massive numbers we have in our prisons.[40]

From 1976 to 1996, the overall budget for the State of Illinois rose 220 percent. The education budget rose 180 percent. The budget for prisons rose 804 percent—not counting capital construction.[41] Illinois increased its prison population ten-fold over a thirty-year period, and during that time prison expenditures rose 1,800 percent, including prison construction costs. A report on the system noted "a disappointingly high recidivism rate."[42] The cost of maintaining a prisoner in Illinois varied from $18,500 to $36,000 per year. By contrast, room and board, student tuition, and fees at the University of Illinois for the 2002–3 school year were $13,096, and at Southern Illinois University, $9,491. South Dakota has closed two of its college campuses and turned them into prisons. In 1982, prisons took 9.5 percent of New York's state budget, and that grew to 24.4 percent by 1997. Most states now spend more money on prisons and prison building than on higher education, though the prison growth rate in 2001 slowed to 1.5 percent nationally. The federal, state, and local governments combined spent more than seven times as much on corrections in the year 2000 as in 1980.

Not only are we wasting money, we are wasting lives—and doing it in a discriminatory fashion. In 2000, 13 percent of the nation's population was African American. They constituted 14 percent of the drug users—and 56 percent of those sentenced to prison for drug-related offenses. In 1980, 143,000 black men were in jail or prison and 463,700 in college. In 2000, 791,600 were incarcerated and 603,032 in college.[43] Figures for Hispanic males are not as dramatically bad, but they also clearly indicate a discriminatory pattern of sentencing.

An in-depth study of juvenile crime sponsored by the National League of Cities, the National Urban League, and other groups concludes: "The changes necessary to win the battle against juvenile crime are not being enacted. Even worse, many local, state and federal leaders have instead been passing laws and funding programs that simply don't work—including some very expensive efforts that may actually increase juvenile crime."[44] Prime examples cited are excessive time served in "correctional institutions" and the increasing frequency of locking up juveniles in adult prisons. As a result of a referendum passed in California in March 2000, it is expected that over a five-year period, 5,600 more young people will be sent to adult prisons who ordinarily would be sent to youth correctional facilities. These young people are much more likely to end up leading a life of crime. Recently, while I was typing this manuscript, a federal judge told me that he had just sentenced a young man to five years in prison because that was what the law mandated. "I should have sentenced him to three months or six months," he said, "but I didn't have that option. He will go into prison a young man who acted foolishly. I fear that in five years he will come out a hardened criminal." The one thing prisoners can learn easily is how to become better criminals.

We have only made our situation worse. In 1999, the Milton Eisenhower Foundation issued a report on crime: "We would not say we had won the war against disease just because we had moved a lot of sick people from their homes to hospital wards. And in a reasonable culture we would not say we have won the war against crime just because we have moved a lot of criminals from the community into prison cells."[45]

Imprisonment *is* the answer for some offenders, particularly those committing crimes of violence. But the applause lines are not always the solid answers. How do you deal with crime if massive incarceration is not the answer? The *real* answers aren't the natural emotional zingers that warm an audience. Solid solutions sound dull and undramatic and slow working, while people yearn for "a silver bullet"—that easy, quick answer. There isn't one. However, there are some things we should try that may not be fast and easy but are potentially more effective.

People who have committed nonviolent crimes perhaps should spend thirty to sixty days in prison to learn its harshness and then be sent to work at a homeless shelter or receive some other assignment that will do them more good, serve society better, and cost the taxpayers less money. All of this must be subject to careful supervision, and if strict rules are not followed by the convicted persons, they should be returned to prison to serve the remainder of their term.

Education is one of the most important considerations. The late Supreme Court justice Warren Burger said, "To confine offenders behind walls without trying to change them is an expensive folly with short-term benefits—winning battles while losing the war."[46] Approximately 81 percent of those in our prisons and jails are high school dropouts, a high percentage of whom are also illiterate. Improve and expand preschool education and later increase the quality and availability of education in grade and high schools, in prisons, and for adults—ex-cons or not—and you will reduce the crime and imprisonment rate. Federal Bureau of Prisons statistics on prisoners released in 1997 show that 84 percent of those in federal prisons who did *not* have a high school diploma or GED (high school equivalency), whether earned in prison or before, ultimately returned to prison. Of those with a high school diploma, 51 percent came back. Of those who had some college, 18 percent returned. When I mentioned these federal statistics to Illinois Department of Corrections director Donald Snyder, he said that state statistics would be similar. Yet Congress cut out federal aid to prisoners who want assistance to take college courses. Why should we give prisoners advantages many responsible citizens don't have? was the argument on the Senate floor, and in the be-tough-on-criminals atmosphere, the restriction passed easily. Late in 2001, the State of Illinois faced a budget crunch caused by the combination of a dipping economy and the aftermath of September 11, and one of the places it became easy to cut was college courses for Illinois prisoners—even though the statistics show that will lead to more crime and eventually to more costs for the taxpayers to house those who commit crimes again. When I asked a U.S. senator who I knew generally had a constructive record on these things why he voted for some harsh federal legislation, he said simply, "I don't want a 30-second commercial attacking me for being soft on crime."

Years ago, when I served in the Illinois General Assembly, I dropped in unannounced at the Vandalia State Prison, then housing 839 inmates. I told the warden I wanted to see the educational facilities. He took me to an empty classroom in a basement with eighteen school desks. He said they used the room every Tuesday evening when an assistant county superintendent of schools came out to teach and "occasionally more than that, because we have one prisoner with a bachelor's degree." That was it! In addition, they had a farm where prisoners worked and acquired some knowledge.

Most states call their bureau of prisons a "Department of Corrections"—but there is little correcting done. In the economic dip of 2001–2, forty-two states found they had to cut their budgets, and many found a politically easy place to make some of those cuts: educational services for prisoners. Prisons are mostly custodial places, where too often gangs operate and youthful offenders learn from more hardened fellow inmates the pathway to a life of crime.

An interest in education doesn't always require a great deal of money. A small program that any community could duplicate is carried on largely by volunteers in the McLean County, Illinois, jail in Bloomington, where inmates serve for less than one year. (To serve more than a one-year sentence, they go to a state prison.) Inmates in the McLean County jail are given the opportunity to read books into a recorder for their children. Then the tapes and small books are sent home for the children to hear their fathers read. It improves reading skills for inmates and lets the children know that their fathers care about them (which the men often say on tape in addition to reading the book). Prisoners and nonprisoners are enthusiastic about the program.[47]

Education isn't the only solution our leaders are ignoring. Shortly before I retired from the U.S. Senate, I visited the Cook County (Chicago) jail, which housed slightly more than nine thousand people that day. As I went through one of the minimum security areas, with cots like my old Army basic training barracks, I asked a prisoner what we could do to help him go straight when he got out. "I want to get into drug treatment," he responded. I turned to the officer showing me around and asked why the inmate could not do that. "We have over nine thousand prisoners and drug treatment for one hundred and twenty men," he responded, to my amazement. The majority of those prisoners were there because of drug offenses or crimes committed as a result of addiction. Roughly 42 percent of state prisoners nationally and 57 percent of federal prisoners are incarcerated because of drug sentences. If you add the crimes committed because of addiction—burglary, for example—these figures escalate. In June 2000, the New York State Commission on Drugs and the Courts reported, "We estimate that last year there were as many as 10,000 non-violent addicted criminal defendants who could have been eligible for treatment, but who were instead sentenced to jail or prison."[48] A Rand Corporation study concluded that drug treatment reduces serious crime approximately fifteen times more than mandatory minimums and ten times more than conventional sentences.[49] New York is trying treatment instead of prison for many drug offenders. The *New York Times* reported: "On average, court-mandated drug treatment programs around the country succeed for 70 percent of those enrolled. In New York City's pilot programs, only 12 percent of the offenders who participated were arrested again, compared to 35 percent of those who did not go through the program."[50]

People who need and want help to break their drug habits should get it, wherever they are. Hospitals with excellent addiction assistance programs have in many instances reluctantly closed them because of the high costs and low reimbursement. Many would be surprised to learn that under President Richard Nixon we had some of our more enlightened crime-fighting policies. In his administration, two-thirds of federal drug money went into treatment and education, one-third into punishment and interdiction. Our nation's drug use declined. Since that time, the ratio has reversed, and while there has been a recent reduction in adult usage, teenage drug habits continue to climb. During my Senate years and now as a faculty member at Southern Illinois University, I find myself counseling young people and often their parents after a drug problem has them in legal difficulty. It is always a discouraging—sometimes heartbreaking—session. Drug education and treatment at all levels can help and should be offered.

Another area we have ignored is our treatment of those with mental illness, something that also impacts the number we house in our prisons. The fifty states saw that keeping 600,000 people in state mental hospitals restricted many who could, with assistance, live a fairly normal life on the outside, and it wasted money. So the states reduced the number in state mental institutions from 600,000 to 50,000, on the theory that community mental health services would be available. In far too many instances, that has not happened, and even where those facilities exist, many of the former patients are not mentally disciplined enough to show up at their allotted appointment times. The result is that many with mental illness are on our streets, receiving no help, and many end up in prisons and jails. At least 270,000—perhaps 500,000—of those in our prisons and jails are in serious need of mental health services. Most are not receiving help.

Even something as fundamental as finding out if a prisoner has a learning disability and therefore cannot read and write is not widely done, although it is vital to that person's achieving a stable future on the outside. When money in a state budget gets tight, an easy place to cut is in prison services, particularly mental health, where the results are not as visible as a mended broken arm. Each year, the nation releases from prisons and jails the equivalent of the population of Seattle (roughly half a million), and many of them are a danger to themselves and to society because they received no rehabilitation while incarcerated.

The direct costs to the taxpayers are enormous. It costs approximately \$20,000 to \$35,000 to incarcerate someone for a year, depending on the nature of the prison and the jurisdiction. The Public Policy Institute at Southern Illinois University, with which I am affiliated, recommended to the courts that whenever people are sentenced, the judge should at the same time indicate the cost to the taxpayers of that imprisonment, tempering the zeal to "lock 'em up and throw away the key." A few court jurisdictions have considered the idea, but this commonsense approach so far has not captured much support.

Almost any judge will tell you in private conversation that he or she has had to be party to a miscarriage of justice because federal and state lawmakers have imposed mandatory sentences for a variety of crimes. Supreme Court Chief Justice William Rehnquist has noted that mandatory minimums often result in warped justice. One federal judge explained to me that he contemplated resigning. He had a young man from a poor, inner-city family before him who, under the mandatory sentencing statute, had to be sentenced to ten years in prison. He had pled guilty. "If he had been a white young man from the suburbs with a good lawyer, he would have been sent somewhere for drug treatment," the judge told me. Sentencing guidelines created by judges themselves are fine, permitting some consistency in sentencing in place of mandatory minimums in the law, but where the circumstances warrant deviation from those guidelines, a judge should be permitted to explain the reason and not be held to a rigid formula. Perhaps a hopeful sign: Iowa in 2001 passed a bill giving judges greater discretion in sentences on drug, property, and burglary crimes.

In 1840, a British leader observed: "Captain Maconochie [a prison reform advocate] avows his opinion that the first object of all convict discipline should be the reformation of the criminal. This opinion, however agreeable it may be to the dictates of humanity, is not, I believe, the received one of legislators, who rather require as the first object of convict discipline that it should be a terror to evildoers."[51] The same zeal to strike terror in evildoers caused the British to have public hangings of pickpockets. As the large crowds gathered, other pickpockets went through the mass of people, collecting their loot.

Stiff mandatory sentences are a combination of wanting to strike terror in evildoers and desiring to get reelected by not crossing public opinion.

Most importantly, we need to work more closely with our young people to keep them out of trouble. School officials and community leaders know when young people are headed for trouble. Those youth need comprehensive attention, and the longer it is delayed, the more expensive it will be for society and for them. Letting them simply drift into further trouble is good for no one.

When difficulties become severe enough to require sentencing, the experience of states tells us that young people sent to large facilities are highly likely to be reincarcerated, with rates varying from 59 percent to 91 percent. Missouri limits its juvenile correction facilities to thirty-three beds, except for three larger institutions. The rate of return within one year has been 11 percent, and over a period of three years, 28 percent violated their parole restrictions. That is not great, but it is much better than the record for the larger facilities most states have.

Some will say that the recent drop in violent crimes in the nation is due to greater rates of incarceration. Measurement is difficult, but as precisely as we can know, the increased incarceration rate is a very small part of the decrease in crime. What is responsible?

More jobs. People who have a chance to get a job are much less likely to commit crime. This is the biggest reason for change.

More education. A higher percentage of our young people are graduating from high school and acquiring additional schooling. More education means more job opportunities and less crime.

Stiffer gun laws. From the issue of who can become a gun dealer to the passage of the Brady bill to licensing handgun owners, and from somewhat stronger enforcement of the gun laws to fewer guns in the hands of irresponsible citizens, all of this means less crime.

Research by the National Academy of Sciences concluded that tripling the time served for violent crimes has "very little" impact on the crime rate.[52] The length of imprisonment appears to have minimal retardant effect; it is rather the sureness and the swiftness of imprisonment that helps. In his excellent book *Race to Incarcerate*, Marc Mauer points out that someone convicted of burglary in the United States serves an average of 16.2 months in prison, while in Canada it is 5.3 months and in England 6.8 months.

From 1980 to 1995, the violent crime rate in the United States per 100,000 citizens went up 15 percent, while the number of state prisoners rose 168 percent.[53] Does locking up more prisoners have an effect on crime? Some argue that it actually increases crime by making more hardened criminals; but it is probable that there is a relationship between putting people in prison and reducing crime, although it appears to be tiny indeed. A study for the British government suggested that increasing the prison population by 25 percent would result in a drop in the crime rate of approximately 1 percent.[54]

Where do we stand today? A Justice Department study released in June 2002 found an increasing rate of crime upon release by those who have been committed to state prisons. Only about 15 percent of state prisoners are enrolled in some type of education or rehabilitation program while incarcerated. Criminologists believe the Justice Department survey suggests that with the longer sentences the other 85 percent are also learning something: how to become "better" criminals.[55] There has to be another course.

Gambling

Why has casino gambling suddenly spread from Las Vegas and Reno to a majority of states? It is not that public opinion is pushing it; most polls show that a majority oppose its spread. What appeals to governors and state legislators and local officials is the promise of increased revenue, with no new taxes—and the gambling leaders say they will be generous at campaign time, and they are. Gambling is the only addiction promoted by government, with the exception of export tobacco sales.

What harm does a little gambling do? If it is "a little," probably no harm, but the campaign contributions don't flow from the gambling gentry so that you can play poker in your home or gamble "a little."

Among addicted gamblers, the attempted suicide rate is many times the national average, and for spouses of compulsive gamblers, it is also well above the national average.[56] Joseph Califano, a former U.S. cabinet member and now the chair of the National Center on Addiction and Substance Abuse at Columbia University, told a gathering there:

> Studies of pathological gamblers reveal that about half are either alcohol or drug abusers. Conversely, among patients in substance abuse treatment, up to 14 percent have been estimated as pathological gamblers, a rate nearly 10 times the rate among the general population. . . . It is also notable that the fastest growing types of gambling are those that appear to be the most addictive, such as slot machines, video poker and video keno. . . . Studies estimate that about 2.5 million adults have met the criteria for pathological gambling in the past year [2001]. More alarming is the fact that 1.1 million adolescents between the ages of 12 and 18 are estimated to be pathological gamblers.[57]

In a conversation with me, financial wizard Warren Buffett called gambling "a tax on stupidity." Medical and other warnings are abundant, but the lure is clear. *U.S. News and World Report* had a dramatic cover: "America's Gambling Fever: How Casinos Empty Your Wallet."[58] But few gamblers will read the message. According to a researcher at the University of California in San Diego, Americans spend 6 percent of their national income on gambling and 8 percent on groceries.[59] John Warren Kindt of the University of Illinois, who has made extensive studies on the gambling industry, writes: "Virtually all pathological gamblers commit crimes, but most are not prosecuted because the crimes are against family members or close associates. . . . Between 12.5 percent and 15 percent of pathological gamblers will become incarcerated."[60] Bankruptcies and divorces increase near casinos. Art Schlichter, quarterback for the Indianapolis Colts, became a gambling addict and ended up owing $1 million at the age of twenty-three. He told NBC: "I remember delivering $60,000 to those guys in a brown paper bag. One of them took the bag and said, 'If it's one dollar short, I'm going to break your arm.'"[61] Schlichter stole his wife's wedding ring and hocked it, and he went from being on the cover of *Sports Illustrated* to becoming a prison inmate. A report by Consumer Credit of Des Moines, Iowa, notes: "It is not coincidental that in 1995 [after the casinos opened in Iowa] the United States experienced a 12% increase in personal bankruptcy versus 1994, while Iowa's numbers shot up 22%. In 1996, the U.S. experienced a 26 percent increase in personal bankruptcy versus 1995. Iowa's numbers ballooned 34 percent. All this during a time that Iowa's economy and employment were far better than the average numbers in the U.S."[62] In a speech in Washington, D.C., Ralph Nader called the gambling industry "even more brazen" than the tobacco and alcohol industries. He charged their marketing efforts were designed to get young people hooked on gambling. He added: "Gambling has a huge history of destroying societies. If you look at the indices for social decay, widespread gambling, historically, is one of the most reliable ones."[63] A method used by the gentry of gambling—they prefer a more sanitized word: *gaming*—to hook minors is the Internet, a difficult mechanism to control since it crosses national boundaries.

The late Msgr. John Egan, an influential Roman Catholic leader in the Chicago area, in an article titled "State-Sanctioned Gambling Is a Bad Bet," wrote, "Of the three major addictions that plague U.S. families—alcohol, drugs, and gambling—gambling is far and away the fastest growing."[64]

The easy-money gambling overlords are not content to get their legislation by simply making campaign contributions. Legislators in five states have been convicted or indicted for accepting bribes. Former Louisiana Governor Edwin Edwards accepted $400,000 in new $100 bills, which he said was a consulting fee; but the jury did not believe him, and he is now in a federal prison in Fort Worth, Texas.

JoDean Joy says she naively voted for a state constitutional amendment that allowed gambling in Deadwood, South Dakota. "I had no idea it would turn out to be 84 casinos in this tiny town. Legalized gambling has put a veneer on the community. The town looks good, but tax dollars will never cover the costs of what the industry is doing to society. It has made for a much more transient community. It has brought jobs, but basically a lot of minimum wage jobs that really haven't contributed to the community's stability."[65] The magazine article that quotes her notes that families are losing homes because of gambling addictions and adds, "Most of the town's businesses are gone—only a grocery and one small hardware store remain." In the small town of Zeigler, Illinois, two men intent on gambling robbed a seventy-two-year-old man and then killed him and burned his house. These are isolated incidents, but the national pattern is clear. Because of big campaign contributions—and sometimes bribes—public officials have created a menace in our midst.

I cannot blame Native American tribal leaders, desperate for money to stem problems of health, alcohol, and unemployment on reservations, and I understand why an extremely poor city like East St. Louis accepts a casino. But national policy should find better answers for both concerns. Lotteries have been part of our history, though the sophisticated casinos are a new development. George Washington approved a lottery to develop the District of Columbia—and even Harvard College got a lift from a lottery. Lotteries disproportionately tax the poor, but they do not tend to be addictive.

But the pervasiveness and addictiveness of today's gambling is a far cry from Washington's small lottery. Gambling survives and thrives because of pandering to these big contributors by public officials. Rosemont, Illinois, population 4,224, happens to be next to O'Hare Airport and Chicago. Mayor Don Stephens wants to put a casino there. During a five-year period, the gambling czars contributed over $430,000 to his campaigns. Not bad for a small town mayor! *Chicago Sun-Times* columnist Mark Brown comments, "The gambling industry is becoming the biggest single player in financing political campaigns in Illinois, and certainly somebody must see how unhealthy that is for our government."[66]

Senator Dan Coats, Republican of Indiana—now our U.S. ambassador to Germany—in 1998 drafted an amendment to an education bill that would have eliminated the ability of wealthy gamblers to deduct their losses before paying taxes, a measure that would have raised $3.8 billion. But five days after he introduced his amendment, Steve Wynn of Mirage Resorts in Las Vegas gave the National Republican Senate Campaign Committee $250,000, and the chairman of the campaign committee announced he would fight the Coats proposal if it were introduced on the floor. Senator Coats saw the writing on the wall and modified his amendment to eliminate the gambling provision. Of the $3.8 billion that would have been saved, $388 million would have come from millionaires.[67] The net result: taxpayer subsidies for millionaire (and other) gambling losses.

Financing Campaigns

Pandering to the whims of public opinion is compounded by the dangers of pandering to those who finance political campaigns. Thomas Jefferson and Alexander Hamilton differed on who should be permitted to vote. Jefferson favored giving all citizens the right to vote, while Hamilton said that people of wealth and property should have the greater voice. Fortunately, Jefferson won that battle, even though we restricted the right to vote for African Americans, Native Americans, and women. But because our system now gives much greater power to those who finance our campaigns, Hamilton has, in fact, prevailed. Even without the campaign finance advantage, people of greater economic standing will have a political advantage because they generally have a better education and are more likely to mix in social circles with decision makers. Some spend huge amounts of their own money to secure public office, the most dramatic example being Mayor Michael Bloomberg of New York City, who spent over $70 million of his own money during the campaign to secure that post, more than the British did in their last national election.

No seeker of major political office is being honest with you if he or she says that political contributions have no impact on conduct. I have never promised anyone a thing for a campaign contribution, but I cannot tell you that I have been unaffected by them. In my autobiography, I wrote:

> When I still served in the Senate and got to my hotel room at midnight, there might be twenty phone calls waiting for me, nineteen from people whose names I did not recognize, the twentieth from someone who gave me a $1,000 campaign contribution or raised money for me. At midnight I'm not going to make twenty phone calls. I might make one. Which one do you think I will make? So will every other incumbent Senator. That means that the financially articulate have inordinate access to policymakers. Access spells influence. The problem permeates our government and too often dictates what we do.[68]

Members of Congress have more fiscal restraints on their personal finances now than at any time in our history, and old-fashioned bribery is probably at an all-time low. Senator Daniel Webster told the banks that if they didn't pay him his legal fee, he would not introduce their legislation. Today, he would be removed from the Senate for such an action. But the public sees huge sums donated to candidates—particularly incumbent candidates—and draws the sometimes accurate conclusion that legislation is for sale. In an earlier era in our nation, railroads "bought" state legislative bodies for land favors the railroads wanted. A crude corruption occasionally marked other early law-making. Now the corruption is generally not crude; it is sophisticated, and the reward is not great personal largess but the ability to stay in office, or to get elected to office. And trust in Congress is at a lower point than in the old days of more brazen, illegal corruption.

One current reason for this lack of trust is the scandal surrounding the Enron Corporation. Because of its legal difficulties, we are learning more about how Enron influenced policy. Here is the seventh paragraph in a *Chicago Sun-Times* report:

> The Clinton and Bush administrations have lobbied India for approval of an Enron project. Four days before India acquiesced, Enron gave $100,000 to the Democratic Party. The Clinton administration even threatened to cut aid to Mozambique, one of the world's poorest nations, if it did not award a pipeline contract to Enron.[69]

During his two senatorial races, Attorney General John Ashcroft received $60,499 from the Enron Corporation's political action committees and top employees. Of the members of the House Energy and Commerce Committee, fifty-one of fifty-six members received contributions from either Enron or Arthur Andersen, the accounting firm implicated in Enron's collapse. The other committee of jurisdiction in the House had forty-nine of its seventy members as recipients. Senate figures are similar, with the two committees being smaller but the amount of contributions larger. How do people such as the attorney general and House and Senate members handle this? Because of the publicity, I am confident there will be no lack of proper attention to Enron's problems. But Enron was seventy-sixth among the large corporations in its donations. What about the others whose activities have not made the national news? It is fair to say they are treated well. They will receive a good return on their investments.

In one of my last days of Senate service in 1996, we had a good (or, more accurately, bad) illustration of how the system works. When the House and Senate disagree on the language of a proposal, there has to be a conference between a few members from each side. Because they are frequently last-minute matters, sometimes things happen in haste but usually not by accident. In one of those conferences, Federal Express got an amendment adopted that classified thirty thousand truck drivers as pilots for labor-management legal purposes, not a move designed to help the truck drivers. The *Washington Post* reported that the company had contributed $1.4 million to incumbent House and Senate members during that two-year cycle. Three of us—Senator Ted Kennedy of Massachusetts, Senator Russ Feingold of Wisconsin, and I—tried to stop the amendment on the floor, without success. I brought the matter up in the Democratic caucus and said that the amendment might have merit, but let's hold hearings and have some research but not pass it without study and not cave in to this special interest. One of my senior colleagues arose in the caucus and said, "Paul's always talking about special interest, special interest, special interest. We have to pay attention to who is buttering our bread."

That tells the story. Money does not always prevail, but usually it does. And candidates with the most money almost always win elections. In the 2000 general election, 93 percent of the Senate and House candidates who spent the most money won. Seventy percent of all the money raised from individuals came from political contributions of $1,000 or more, given by one-seventh of 1 percent of our population. Does it pay off for them? You bet. And most of them will candidly admit that. Alexander Hamilton must be chuckling in his grave.

I favor a system of public financing of campaigns, but as long as the present practice exists, it is important that citizens without an economic axe to grind contribute to worthy candidates. Even the $5 or $10 contribution helps to offset other donors less well motivated. Another effective way of balancing the big dollars is to be a volunteer. Officeholders pay attention to those who do the important but undramatic work of stuffing envelopes, knocking on doors, researching issues, and the other essentials of a campaign. But the dollar curse of elections remains a serious affliction.

Here's a striking example from two decades ago. In the 1980s, the proposal to build B-2 bombers faced us; the Air Force opposed making them, as did the Pentagon. They cost $1.4 billion each. The California manufacturer thoughtfully placed subcontracts around the nation, and the subcontractors and their labor unions contacted members of the House and Senate in behalf of a bomber the Air Force didn't want. It meant jobs back home. Members of the House and Senate also knew that if they voted for the B-2 bomber, in all likelihood they would receive campaign contributions, and if they didn't vote for it, they would not. We ended up with the B-2 bombers. As I write this, the Senate has passed the appropriations for defense for FY 2003, and it includes $3.3 billion to buy fifteen C-17 transport planes, three more than the Pentagon requested, and forty-eight F/A018 carrier-based Hornet fighter-bombers for $9.2 billion, four more planes than the Pentagon wanted. The fingerprints of campaign contributions are all over the budget.

Secretary of Defense Donald Rumsfeld is trying to cancel a cannon, called the Crusader—the worst possible name at a time of Christian-Muslim tensions. It is too bulky for effective mobile use, but many members of Congress and the manufacturer and the subcontractors are at work to push it through—and the invisible lobbyist in all of this is the campaign contribution. Will it prevail?

Bill Moyers puts it bluntly: "The soul of democracy has been dying, drowning in a rising tide of big money contributed by a narrow, unrepresentative elite that has betrayed the faith of citizens in self-government."[70] What happens when public opinion polls and campaign contributors are on opposite sides? Usually—but not always—money wins. Polls show, for example, that two-thirds of the public favors a system to guarantee universal health care access. That ordinarily would carry the day. But in 1999–2000, the medical supply people donated $4.5 million in campaign contributions and spent $12.1 million for lobbying activities. The health professional groups gave $5.4 million in campaign contributions and spent $49.1 million lobbying. The pharmaceutical manufacturers donated $18.9 million to campaigns and paid $67.9 million lobbying Congress. The health insurance industry donated $9.9 million to federal candidates and spent $35.8 million for the service of lobbyists. With few exceptions, people in these industries much prefer the status quo to a system guaranteeing universal coverage. With 43 million Americans without health insurance coverage, candidates who make this a big issue can have a substantial public following—but they also deprive themselves of money that is needed to win a campaign. In a choice between receiving campaign dollars or seeing that a popular move to guarantee health care to all Americans gets enacted, Congress chooses the money.

It always seems to be about money at some level. In 1999 and 2000, the United States got into a mini–trade war with Western Europe over bananas, of all things. Do we grow bananas in the United States for export sale? No. Of the hundreds of requests to the U.S. trade representative, we choose about fourteen products annually to take to an international trade court. In 1996, we chose bananas as one of them. Why were we fighting the Europeans on bananas? The chief executive officer of Chiquita is Carl Lindner, who in 2000 and 2001 headed efforts to get the Europeans to lift their quotas on bananas. In 2000, he contributed $550,000 to the Republican Party and at least $270,000 to the Democrats. Over the decade, he contributed more than $5 million to the two political parties.[71] On April 11, 1996, the U.S. trade representative filed a formal case with the World Trade Organization on bananas. On April 12—the next day—Lindner and his top executives "began funneling more than $500,000 to Democratic Party Committees in about two dozen states that were key battlegrounds for that year's presidential election."[72] Lindner slept in the Lincoln bedroom. At a live television broadcast from Ford's Theatre in Washington, D.C., the following exchange took place in which comedian Paula Poundstone was featured:

Poundstone: What determines who gets which seat? . . . Do you know who that is behind your head?

Hostess Seated Next to President Clinton: Carl Lindner.

Poundstone: Carl Lindner. I'm sorry, I'm not familiar. What made you give him that seat? [Laughter]

Hostess: A whole lot of money. [Laughter]

Poundstone: A whole lot of money! [Applause and laughter] . . . Carl, why do you have so much money? [Laughter] . . . What do you do for a living? . . . Mr. President, do you know who Carl Lindner is? [Laughter]

Clinton: [Nods yes]

Poundstone: Would you mind telling me?

Clinton: It's a secret. [Laughter]

Clinton: He's in bananas, sort of like you are.

Poundstone: He's in bananas! . . . He's what? He's the Chiquita banana guy! . . . Without the fruit on your head, sir, I didn't recognize you. [Laughter and applause] . . . Why does the President know the banana guy?[73]

Poundstone's comedy routine was more insightful than she realized.

In another instance, between 1993 and 1999, one racetrack owner in Illinois contributed $1.46 million to state political leaders. In 1999, a bill passed and became law providing changes that give that racetrack $17.2 million in assistance.

I usually disagree with Rush Limbaugh, but when the *National Review* asked him if he would ever run for office, he replied: "I have no desire [to do it]. Primarily because . . . to be elected to anything, you have to walk around like this—with your hand out. And you have to beg people to put something in it. Somebody always does, and they want repayment. And not with dollars. It's going to be with your soul, it's going to be with a portion of your soul. I don't look at it as fun."[74]

Or listen to another conservative who became famous for speaking his mind, Senator Barry Goldwater: "To be successful, representative government assumes that elections will be controlled by the citizenry at large, not by those who give the most money. Electors must believe their votes count. Elected officials must owe their allegiance to the people, not to their own wealth or the wealth of interest groups who speak only for the selfish fringes of the whole community."[75]

Former Congressman Paul Findley (R-Illinois) relates approaching an Ohio colleague on the floor of the House, asking him how he would vote on a pending measure. He responded: "I haven't yet been financially advised."[76] Political observer Bill Moyers puts it bluntly: "If a baseball player was to hand money to an umpire we would call it a bribe. With politicians we call it a contribution."[77]

The long arm of campaign contributions reaches into unexpected places—and sometimes, those of us critical of our present system may be incorrect in our conclusions. Legislators may believe how they vote is in the national interest. Because of the aura that this crude method of financing campaigns provides, we on occasion may make inaccurate judgments. But far too often, it is difficult to find any answer other than that campaign money dictated decisions.

The effects of these contributions are sometimes felt far beyond our own shores. In July 2001, the United Nations had a conference on the illegal trade in small arms, an illicit trade that is said to cause half a million deaths a year around the world. The United States is by far the largest producer and seller of arms, though we have tighter control on their sale outside of our country than most nations have. Sixty-eight percent of our arms sales are to developing nations. When the United Nations met to see what could be done to stop the illegal sales, the United States refused to cooperate because, we said, such cooperation would violate the Second Amendment of our Constitution. Any third-rate lawyer will tell you that is not the case. What did cause our action? Many believe it was the contributions of the arms manufacturers. The *Bulletin of the Atomic Scientists* notes, "In 1999, the last year for which full statistics are available, the United States was responsible for 54 percent of international arms deliveries—more than all other supplier nations in the world combined."[78] Others say the political pressure and contributions of the National Rifle Association did it. Whatever the cause, it hardly made a ripple in the U.S. news scene but did not help our image in other nations. And it did not help innocent people who are, almost without notice, killed each day around the world.

Or look at this headline: "After U.S. Objects, World Fails to Agree to Curb Smoking Ads." The article notes: "Saying tobacco is responsible for the deaths of an estimated four million people a year, the World Health Organization has tried hard to encourage its 191 member countries to agree on measures to reduce significantly the use of tobacco. . . . The American positions drew a chorus of criticism from antismoking advocates, who insisted that the Bush administration was echoing tobacco industry stands, an argument that the senior American delegate . . . firmly denied. No American officials commented after the conclusion of the talks."[79] Is our position dictated by contributions of U.S. tobacco companies? Many people believe so.*

Elizabeth Drew writes, "The greatest change in Washington in the last twenty-five years—in its culture, in the way it does busi-

*Eighteen months later, in May 2003, the United States suddenly and without explanation reversed its stand to support the international anti-smoking endeavor.

ness, and the ever-burgeoning amount of business transactions that go on here—has been the preoccupation with [political] money."[80]

Thanks to the doggedness of Senators John McCain and Russ Feingold, and thanks to the Enron scandal, with its embarrassing campaign funding disclosures, the nation took a step forward on campaign finance reform, but we have a long path ahead yet. New York University scholar Burt Neuborne, after lengthy studies, ends one of his articles with these words: "Ask yourselves one question: Is this the democracy I want to pass on to my children? If it's not you owe it to yourselves and to your children to try to rescue democracy from the sludge of money, power, and influence that threaten its vitality and moral power. Structural reform of the way we finance democracy is the only way out."[81]

A few states are pioneering in significant improvements. Arizona and Maine now have a one-election experience with public financing of campaigns. Arizona found they had 60 percent more candidates, 62 percent more contests, and a higher voter turnout. Maine had similar experiences, and 54 percent of the "clean election" (i.e., publicly financed) candidates won. Candidates found the big difference in campaigning was that they were spending more time talking to the electorate, not so much time on the phone pleading for funds. A move toward having limited free radio and television time for major candidates is gathering steam and is mentioned in more detail in the next chapter.

The problem of campaign contributions is not only with Congress. Had Attorney General Janet Reno decided to name an independent counsel to look into campaign donation improprieties, instead of the Monica Lewinsky matter, we would have had shattering headlines about campaign contributions in the Clinton administration and their direct connection to public policy. And maybe reforms. The president of ABC asked President Lyndon Johnson, sometimes not our most sensitive leader, to have a fund-raiser at the White House for the Kennedy Center. Johnson replied that he "didn't want to start raising funds at the White House—even for the Red Cross or United Fund, because one person . . . in the room could . . . have something pending in Congress and they'd say he was buying his way into the White House."[82] Since Johnson's day, we have become accustomed to the use of the White House for fund-raising, but that is a small, visible part of the abuse. To the extent that there is public interest in this issue, credit must be given to Senator John McCain in his quest for the Republican presidential nomination. He daily and hourly stressed the importance of campaign finance reform.

While we hope to see changes in the future, we are seeing few improvements in the short term. The *Wall Street Journal*'s lead article of March 6, 2001, has the heading: "Industries That Back Bush Are Now Seeking Return on Investment." The story starts, "For the businesses that invested more money than ever before in George W. Bush's costly campaign for the presidency, the returns have already begun."[83] Unless you read the *Wall Street Journal*, you did not hear about it. No big news. We have come to expect that.

A few states have initiated campaign finance reforms, and the area that may lead the way to national reform is public financing of judicial campaigns. The Committee on Judicial Independence of the American Bar Association is on record favoring that, and the public recognizes that it is somehow unseemly for lawyers to contribute to judicial elections and then appear before those same judges in a trial or in an appeal. But the practice should be equally offensive in lawmaking by legislators.

Exceptions

What about cases in which most legislators are clearly not following public opinion and the polls and the campaign money? There are such examples.

I spoke at a church-sponsored event in Decatur, Illinois, and someone in the audience asked, "Why does Congress follow the wishes of the National Rifle Association so faithfully when public opinion polls show a majority of the public favors sensible gun legislation?" I asked how many in the audience of perhaps one hundred fifty people had written to their House and Senate members in the last six months asking for "sensible gun legislation"? Not a hand was raised. Two percent of the population that pays attention to an issue will ordinarily prevail over 98 percent who pay no attention. I am not suggesting that the NRA's position has that small a portion of public support, but they are clearly in the minority. However, they write and write and write to their legislators. They are generous with campaign contributions. They are effective.

Or take another issue, support for the United Nations. Until shortly after September 11, when the United States hastily paid much of its arrearage to the United Nations, 81 percent of the past-due amount owed to that organization was owed by the United States. One author accurately sums up our situation: "Although public opinion strongly . . . supports the UN . . . it has little bite because it lacks electoral consequences. Voters do not cast ballots based on their own or on candidates' views about the UN."[84] There is a United Nations Association—to which I belong—but most members I meet are my age (seventy-four) or near that, and the group does not take such elemental steps as keeping in touch with young people who participate in Model UN programs, which hold mock UN sessions for students to "represent" various nations and learn how the United Nations works. The United Nations Association is a group of well-intentioned people but one that has not attempted to develop political muscle. There is another small but rigid and noisy group of people who oppose the United Nations, and until the September 11 crisis, when we needed world support, Congress found no political liability in ignoring our UN obligations.

Putting the squeeze on UN activities is popular with that small group, led particularly by those in Congress who know nothing about the United Nations, which keeps peace in the Sinai and in Cyprus and which in a thousand other ways helps our world move toward becoming more stable and more civilized. Listening to some of the speeches, it sounds as if the organization has huge amounts of money that it throws around recklessly. Its operating budget has stayed small for years, $1.25 billion. That is "half the budget of South Dakota, or $600 million less than that of the Tokyo fire department."[85] The United States hampers UN activities in other ways also, to appease the UN-haters in Congress who are trying to satisfy the small, noisy anti-UN public fringe group. Most supporters of the United Nations don't contact their members. The anti-UN people do.

Clearly, if an informed public became more vocal about their wishes in these and other areas, the votes of officeholders might be different, might be more responsible. We must each become engaged and become part of the dialogue that helps shape our destiny.

Examples of Courage

The picture is not all bleak, of course. Presidential leadership can make a difference, as can a strong governor. And there are individual acts of heroism that go largely unnoted.

Senator Henry Bellmon, a Republican from Oklahoma, was elected governor of that state in 1962 and then went to the U.S. Senate in 1969. The national press hardly noticed Bellmon because of his low-key style. Members on both sides of the aisle respected him and knew that he tried to vote and work for the best interest of the nation. He became the top Republican on the Senate Budget Committee, and because of his close work with the Democratic chairman, Senator Edmund Muskie of Maine, most budget problems on the Senate side got solved without rancor and usually with a unanimous vote of the Budget Committee. Because both Muskie and Bellmon were regarded highly by their colleagues, Senate resolutions on the budget passed with little controversy. On the House side, partisanship played a much stronger role and achieving agreement on a budget did not come easily.

Then the inflammatory issue of the Panama Canal Treaty emerged, negotiated in large part by the former chief executive of Xerox, Ambassador Sol Linowitz, who had a great combination of practicality and diplomatic skill. Particularly in the southern and near-south states, public opinion was being molded by the American Legion and other groups that strongly opposed "giving up the Panama Canal." Our real national interest was to keep the canal open for shipping, and as Roman Catholic Archbishop Marcus McGrath, the leading religious figure in Panama, pointed out, if we did not approve a treaty giving the Panamanian people control over the canal in their country, we would be playing into the hands of the Communists and other extremists and jeopardizing our continued use of the canal. Henry Bellmon knew all of this, and he understood the clear national interest. He also knew that if he voted for the Panama Canal Treaty, he might not get reelected. He talked with some of us about his dilemma. When the time came for that crucial vote, he supported the treaty—and shortly after that announced that he would not be a candidate for reelection to the Senate, where he enjoyed serving and had served the nation well. Polls in Oklahoma showed 90 percent of the people opposed to the treaty. After his vote, the largest newspaper in the state called Bellmon a traitor—a man who had served as a marine during World War II and participated in several landings, including the costly landing at Iwo Jima. Bellmon and Senator Howard Baker of Tennessee were the only southern Republicans who supported the treaty. It passed with one vote to spare. Years later, Bellmon wrote in his autobiography: "It is a perversion of the public trust for an elected official to act against the public interest in order to retain office. Legislators who claim to always do their constituents' will are in effect trying to follow rather than lead."[86] The political heat on this issue gradually diminished, and seven years later, the voters of Oklahoma chose him as their governor again.

Another example: the late Senator Paul Wellstone and changes in the welfare system. Everyone is for welfare reform. Those who are on welfare know it needs to be changed, those who administer the programs know the same, and the taxpayers who foot the bill sense that modification of policies is desirable, even though there is an exaggerated view of what the dollar costs are.

So when President Bill Clinton and the Republican leadership of Congress agreed on "welfare reform," public opinion overwhelmingly supported the proposal. It contained a provision that people on welfare could get federal subsidies for no more than a total of five years, from the date of the enactment of the proposal, with states permitted to cut that time shorter. Twenty-two states reduced the time. In practical terms, the law said to a woman with three children living in a large housing project in Chicago or in rural Mississippi that in five years or less from the date of the enactment of the legislation she could no longer draw any federal dollars for welfare—and there was no provision in the law for a job, or for job training, or for day care for children.

Some of the antiwelfare talk has a mixture of frustration and racism, and those who supported the proposal pointed to the declining number of recipients on welfare even before the deadline. Many observers, however, believe the improved economy, which gave greater employment opportunities to those of limited skills, was the main cause of the decline. But there is no question that some moved off welfare to become even poorer.

What I believe to be a sensible answer—and in some ways a tougher answer—is to have a federal jobs program for those who cannot find work in the private sector, modeled after the Works Progress Administration (WPA) of the FDR days. I proposed requiring people to work, not after five years but after five weeks, unless they had small children or suffered from a disability. They would be paid for working four days a week at the minimum wage, not a great deal of money but more than the average family receives on welfare in all but three states. On the fifth day, they would have to be out trying to find a job in the private sector. My proposal also called for requiring that those who cannot read and write to enter literacy programs; those without a high school diploma or a GED would be required to attempt to get one if they have the ability; and those without a marketable skill would be encouraged to enter a community college or technical school to acquire one. I discussed this idea with President Clinton, and he seemed to like it, and then he asked the natural question: How much would it cost? I told him the estimate for the first year would be $12 billion, with declining costs after the first year. That dimmed his interest, somewhat understandably, though compared with the multiyear $1.3 *trillion* in tax cuts approved in the first year of the George W. Bush administration, it would have been tiny. This jobs program would do infinitely more good for the nation than the tax cut, which, based on fuzzy and inaccurate projections of revenue, will do us harm. Like the original WPA, a sound jobs program would be a great investment in our people and in our future productivity. But we were looking for something inexpensive that had the label "welfare reform."

Technically labeled "Temporary Assistance for Needy Families," the 1996 "welfare reform" act was fully implemented in late 2002. It requires states to spend 75 percent of what they spent for welfare in 1994 and prohibits the use of federal funds (but not state funds) to a family with an adult receiving welfare for more than five years, stops payments to unmarried minor parents not living in a situation where there is adult supervision, and prohibits payments to certain immigrants. (Some of the measure's deficiencies are becoming apparent, and the House and Senate are looking at changes as I write.)

Two years after the act's passage, the Children's Defense Fund and the National Coalition for the Homeless both reported an increase in the number of homeless in several parts of the nation. Twenty-two states inaugurated a family cap, which the legislation permitted, saying that a woman on welfare could not receive additional payments for more children. A study in New Jersey found that the result in that state has been an increase in the number of abortions by women on welfare and intensified poverty for some women who did not have abortions. The Roman Catholic publication *America* noted editorially that one of the few areas where pro-choice and pro-life advocates agree is that this provision—no additional payments if there are more children—should be repealed.[87] But it was part of the money-saving provision of the law. Shifting people off Medicaid, which most receive under welfare, also saves the states and federal government money but creates desperate situations for many. By 1999—well before the dip in the economy—two million poor families with average annual incomes of about $7,500 had lost 8 percent of their income.[88]

Under the law, the states receive block grants in place of the older welfare programs that were aimed directly at poor families. In the first two years of the new program, states received $34.4 billion, and—because of the drops in welfare numbers, largely because of the improved economy—that exceeded the amount they formerly would have received by about $6 billion. The state that did the most in job placement—and spent the most money per welfare recipient—was Wisconsin, headed by the Republican governor, Tommy Thompson, now the Secretary of Health and Human Resources in the George W. Bush administration. He accurately observed: "I've told Congress, and I've told taxpayers, you can't do this cheaply. You have to spend more in the beginning to save on the back end."[89] Asked about the impact of the law, a health clinic administrator in West Virginia observed: "We will be having more women being arrested. The reason is, they are not going to let their kids go hungry. So they'll steal and we'll build more prisons to house them."[90]

The bipartisan nature of the sponsorship, plus the label of welfare reform, combined with saving money and stopping "those people" from getting welfare benefits, created overwhelming public support for the 1996 law. The chief opponent, Senator Daniel Moynihan of New York, decimated the arguments of supporters of the measure in his remarks on the Senate floor, but that legislative train had so much momentum that it passed the Senate with only twelve votes against it. Only one senator in a race for reelection, the late Paul Wellstone, a Democrat from Minnesota, opposed the measure. He not-so-quietly told his Senate colleagues that the vote might cost him the election, and it became a major issue in television ads and on billboards that called him "Senator Welfare."[91] His opponent called him "embarrassingly liberal." However, to the surprise of many observers, he won—barely—with 49.7 percent, with six minor party candidates in the race in addition to his Republican opponent.

Similarly, Governor Jim Edgar of Illinois, the popular Republican who had formerly served as the secretary of state, faced a contest for reelection against Attorney General Neil Hartigan, a capable and popular Democrat. The previous governor, James Thompson, and the Illinois legislature had enacted a "temporary tax surcharge" in 1989 increasing the state income tax from 2.5 percent to 3 percent for two years, with the increase going to education. During his campaign, Jim Edgar said he would support efforts to make it permanent, because he saw no way to avoid that without harming the schools. Neal Hartigan made a big issue of the tax increase, saying he would provide the money for education with cuts in other unspecified areas and would eliminate the tax surcharge.

Pollsters assembled a small focus group, composed of roughly one-third leaning toward Hartigan, one-third leaning toward Edgar, and one-third undecided. When the Hartigan television commercials were played, attacking Edgar for the tax increase, the assembled group largely agreed with Hartigan, as they did on some other commercials. But when the pollsters asked the group, "Whom do you trust?" the group opinion switched to Edgar. Then they were asked, "For whom would you vote?" And again Edgar won—as he did in the election.[92] Generally, the trust factor wins over individual issues. And trust is not established by simply doing what is popular.

There are other illustrations of courage prevailing. It is not the easy course, but it is the noble course. The ability of members of the U.S. House and Senate is much better than the public perception. The quality that is most lacking is courage. The electorate can play a stronger role by demanding reform of our campaign finance laws and by looking for candidates and officeholders with courage, with vision. Don't go to a physician who tells you just what you want to hear, and don't support a candidate who tells you just what you want to hear.

Since 1777, people who wish to vote in Vermont have had to take the following oath (with only the final word being changed, in modern times, to "person"): "I solemnly swear, by the ever living God (or affirm in the presence of Almighty God), that whenever I am called to give my vote or suffrage, touching any matter that concerns the State of Vermont, I will do it so, as in my conscience, I shall judge will most conduce to be best good of the same, as established by the constitution, *without fear or favor of any man*" (my emphasis).[93] Maybe we should all take that oath, particularly those who hold public office.

2

Pandering in the Media

NBC, ABC and CBS aired 874 O. J. [Simpson] stories in 1995; CNN had broadcast 388 hours of O. J. by the time the jury in the criminal trial began deliberating. . . . More than 1,000 press credentials were issued [for the trial]; one in three U.S. newspapers published special editions for the verdict. . . . Eighteen books about the O. J. trial are available through Amazon.

—"We Went Berserk," *Columbia Journalism Review,* November/December 2001

"We're Giving the Public What It Wants"

It is not difficult to find editorials rightfully criticizing officeholders for actions that are popular but ill-advised. However, editorials are rare indeed that criticize the media for following practices that are popular but do not serve the nation well.

"We're giving the public what it wants" is the pious but lame defense by media executives of such actions. That defense has the same hollow ring to it that irresponsible political leaders use: "I'm representing my people and doing what they want." Pandering in the media primarily is focused on two interrelated objects: first, higher ratings or greater circulation, getting as large an audience as possible; and second, making as much money as possible.

By every measure—time on radio or television, inches in newspapers and news magazines—we saw many times more media coverage of the O. J. Simpson trial than the fall of the Berlin Wall. Which is more significant? To ask the question is to answer it. The Simpson trial titillates us but does nothing to make us more informed citizens. Garrison Keillor told an audience of news people, "When you slip into the field of entertainment, then you will be expected to be fascinating. . . . Nobody can be fascinating for long, but people can be accurate and responsible for an entire career."[1] PBS's Jim Lehrer comments, "Journalism, as practiced by some, has become something akin to professional wrestling—something to watch rather than to believe."[2] Is there anything wrong with television and newspapers and radio entertaining us? No, but when the rating wars on television cause the news to be warped by the entertainment factor, the nation loses. And it is not simply the Simpson trial versus the Berlin Wall juxtaposition.

Marvin Kalb wrote a thoughtful book on the coverage of the Monica Lewinsky incident, *One Scandalous Story: Clinton, Lewinsky, and Thirteen Days That Tarnished American Journal-*

ism. Many would amend the subtitle to "That *Further* Tarnished American Journalism."

Another example of scandalmongering, similar to the coverage given the Clinton-Lewinsky affair, preoccupied the media before the terrorist attack of September 11. Almost every day for eleven weeks, most newspapers and radio and television stations carried accounts of Congressman Gary Condit of California and an intern of his, Chandra Levy, who disappeared. Dan Rather of CBS was a happy exception to the general rule of hyping the story. Matters of national and international importance frequently received little or no attention while we absorbed ourselves in this sex mystery.

Compare that with a problem that will loom large soon: a world water crisis. In one of President Clinton's last days in office, intelligence agencies—including the CIA—gave him their analysis of where the world's supply of fresh water will be in fifteen years. They said that the great resource shortage in the world will not be oil but water, and that there will be regional wars fought over water. The problem is already serious in many areas, and it is a time bomb in the volatile Middle East. In Amman, the capital of Jordan, a city of one million, people are already limited to turning on their water taps one day a week. Israeli Foreign Minister Shimon Peres says that water will be a regional catalyst either for peace or for war. When I've talked to key people in network television, they all agree on the importance of the story, but they add, "It has no sex appeal. People will yawn. It is a dull subject." Their concern is that their ratings will go down. So we get more Gary Condit–type stories. That pleases the business executives and their bookkeepers who are calling the shots in far too much of the media industry. Newspapers have been slightly better on the water issue, and if the newspapers played it up more, television almost inevitably would follow. The Associated Press distributed some good stories, but few newspapers picked them up. *Parade* magazine did a feature story. But among the big media, the most significant exception to the neglect of this topic has been from *National Geographic*. In no other magazine of general circulation has there been such a substantial look at where we're headed.

The sun is setting on the days of family-owned newspapers and radio and television stations. I wish that were not so. More and more people who make the decisions about the number of news personnel and other matters are business types, with limited experience, if any, on the news side. Most of these corporations are publicly held, and those in charge of these corporations understandably want to please the stockholders. If the newspaper or television station is making a 15 percent profit, they want to boost it to 16 percent. Pulitzer prizes are nice, but I sense they're not as important to most of these CEOs as the profit margin, though they know that a good reputation adds to marketability. So news treatment by reporters, who are spread too thin, tends to be superficial. Personal things that would not have made the news thirty or forty years ago often are the big news items. "It's what the public wants," we're told.

A few decades ago, Illinois had a governor whose wife had serious alcohol problems. I saw her fall on her face at a dinner where five hundred or more people had gathered, including perhaps twenty reporters. Everyone in politics and the press corps knew of her addiction, but not a word appeared in the media. Today, its entertainment appeal would bring the story to us with juicy details, crowding out more substantial articles. The attention to the lurid, the sexy, the titillating, and the trivial is the result of media decision makers who too often have the unexpressed motto, If it sells, it's good.

I tell this next incident with apologies, because I have written about it before and told it often, but it illustrates the point so well. During my service in the state legislature, Paul Douglas, a great U.S. senator and my political mentor, called and asked me to introduce a resolution in the Illinois General Assembly urging the U.S. Congress to make the corn tassel the national flower. He would then introduce the measure in the Senate. Because of my great admiration for him, I said yes. But as I reflected on it, I really did not want to do it. That night, I called the senator and asked, "Are you sure you want me to introduce a resolution on the corn tassel? Are you sure you want to introduce a resolution in the Senate?" The professor-turned-senator laughed and responded with a lecture that taught me something about politics and journalism.

"Paul," he said, "if you want to stay in public office you have to get media attention. The substantial things you do generally will not get attention unless they are involved in a major controversy. The media loves trivia. You have to do a certain amount of that to stay alive politically. No one will get angry with you because you want to make the corn tassel the national flower. And don't worry, it will never pass."[3] This excessive attention to the trivial, to the scintillating, is not good for the nation and is not responsible journalism.

Jonathan Alter of *Newsweek* is correct: "There's a big difference between the right to do something—and the right thing to do."[4] One study of network news found that over a twenty-year period, "the proportion of network news stories concerning ethical lapses in Congress more than quadrupled."[5] Does that reflect reality? No. My guess is the ethical lapses were no greater and no less during that twenty years. What happened is that more attention has been given to that type of audience-grabbing news that not only distorts reality but also feeds public cynicism. It is possible that this greater attention to corruption reflects a rising moral standard journalists expect of officeholders. I am sure that is true of some in the media, but my overall impression is that it is primarily a race to win viewers or readers and to win the "gotcha" prize.

The United States still has some of the best media in the world, but pandering to whatever creates a larger audience compromises that quality. The better newspapers, in particular, frequently have in-depth stories that have no immediate financial payoff but are informative and often motivating. In the developing nations and in the new democracies of eastern Europe, in most cases the media is gradually improving, in part because of assistance from U.S.-based groups like the Freedom Forum. My impression is that our media is not as good today as it was ten or twenty years ago, largely because of the reduction in the number of people covering the news. Reporters are better educated than when I started as a journalist, but I find it hard to disagree with Marvin Kalb's assessment: "There is overwhelming evidence that standards continue . . . to fall."[6] The frenzy created by the Monica Lewinsky scandal—legitimate but overcovered news, some of it based on unsubstantiated rumors—stands in contrast to the lack of coverage of a host of significant national and international events. Marvin Kalb produced these amazing statistics on the Monica Lewinsky matter in *responsible* newspapers: On January 25, 1998, the *New York Times* published twenty-one stories, composed of 19,524 words. The *Washington Post* on the same day had the same number of articles and a total of 32,829 words. Two days earlier, the *Los Angeles Times* had twenty stories and 14,152 words.[7] Not surprisingly, television was no better. Even the finest of television's reporter-hosts, Ted Koppel, featured the Lewinsky affair fifteen days in a row on *Nightline*. To the credit of the *Wall Street Journal* and the *Chicago Tribune*, their coverage showed restraint. Almost lost to the public in all the media hype were serious federal budget decisions, a crisis in the Middle East, and increased tensions in Iraq. In the midst of these issues, presidential press secretary Mike McCurry held his regular briefing for reporters, and of the 128 questions he was asked, 113 focused on the Lewinsky matter.[8] Harold Evans, former editor of the *Sunday Times* of London and now a leading U.S. journalist, said—more than a year before we had heard about Monica Lewinsky—"I'm not saying that Paula Jones's pants-dropping suit can be ignored. . . . But it's a question of priority, of perspective, of relevance. I am saying that the frenzy of activity on such questions is grotesquely misapplied when one contemplates what the press is not doing."[9]

What is the media not covering? One example: poverty. We have a higher percentage of our children living in poverty than any of the other wealthy industrial nations. Looking at local television coverage, one study reports: "Out of 8,095 stories studied this year, only seven concerned the disadvantaged. . . . Over three years and some 25,000 stories, only 35 focused on the needy."[10]

What is important is always a subjective judgment. The proclamation of the Declaration of Independence made page 2 of the *Hartford Courant*. But consistent media inattention to basic problems in our society is inexcusable. It breeds discontent and indifference.

Part of the diminished reporting of important news is caused by a reduction in the number of reporters. Television, radio, and newspapers are victims of the shrinkage caused by mergers and the bookkeeping mentality of those who make the big media decisions, people who are not news-oriented but dollar-oriented. The *Chicago Sun-Times*, for example, once had excellent reporters on the Washington scene: Jerome Watson, Basil Talbott, Mike Briggs, Lynn Sweet, and others. Today, the Washington bureau of the *Sun-Times* is one person, Lynn Sweet. She files good copy, but one person cannot do what several formerly did. That is being repeated over and over in television and radio and at other newspapers. In order to save money, the networks pooled their resources for election night and created the Voter News Service, and then they gradually cut its budget. On election night 2000, in the tight Bush-Gore race, Voters News Service called it wrong, and the networks—fueled in part by eagerness to be the first in calling the win—followed their inaccurate, low-budget lead, causing confusion in this nation and around the world.

I have sympathy for an appetite to make money but not for the all-consuming zeal that looks only at the short term. I once published small, weekly newspapers, thirteen of them in four printing plants. I wanted my newspapers to make money or they would fold. I also knew that if those newspapers served their communities well, the communities would prosper, and in the long run, so would the newspapers. I can't *prove* that formula works, but my strong impression is that it does. (I also believe it applies beyond the media field. My investments are modest, but I look for business executives who do things to help their community or a larger interest. If a business leader is willing to look long-term at a community, knowing that what helps that community will ultimately help the business, that leader is also likely to look long-term at his or her business. Using this as part of my formula for buying stocks, I have done much better than Dow Jones or the other indexes.)

A 2001 survey of newspeople by the *Columbia Journalism Review* showed 84 percent of those polled found newsroom morale low, while only 15 percent think it is not low. One of the major reasons: profits taking priority over good reporting. The assistant managing editor of the *Lexington (Kentucky) Herald-Leader* commented, "I would decrease the newspaper's profit requirement—and sprinkle a 'quality' dividend throughout three areas: staffing, training, and travel."[11] In 2000, newspapers cut their staffs by a total of eighteen hundred.[12] Television and radio had the same trend, but I do not know the figures. Did newspapers and radio and television make money? Yes, but the CEOs would tell you, "not enough." Excessive pandering to stockholders is as bad as any other form of pandering. It is of more than passing interest that the major mutual funds that try to invest in socially responsible corporations do not have any newspaper stock.[13] I do, but I buy in companies that I believe are more than money machines. It is important to remember the words of Tim McGuire, who stepped down in mid-2002 as president of the American Society of Newspaper Editors: "We do not make Wheaties and we do not make car bumpers. We make newspapers for a free society."[14] To make profit an all-absorbing pursuit does not serve the nation well, and in the long run, it will not serve the media outlets well. The *New York Times* makes more money than the *National Enquirer*, and to the extent that on rare occasions it mirrors the *Enquirer*, it is not serving its own financial future well. Trust is an important factor in any field. Generally, responsible newspapers are showing circulation gains, not large increases, but gains nevertheless. There are exceptions to that generalization. I agree with Sandra Mims Rowe, editor of the *Oregonian*, who told a convention of the American Society of Newspaper Editors: "The notion that readers have created the demand for lowest common denominator journalism is false. We are doing that ourselves."[15] In England, the percentage of citizens who read newspapers has grown 67 percent since 1970. In the United States, the percentage has declined. In television and radio, the pattern of short-term public response is less clear, but as the education level in the United States gradually rises, responsibility in the media should pay off financially.

Another form of media pandering concerns me. Television and radio editorials—when they rarely occur—are usually bland; typically, they are opposed to sin and for freedom. But too many newspaper editorials are the same, and newspapers do not have a federal license that might be taken away. The unspoken motto that hangs over too many editorial-writing desks is: Don't offend the advertisers. Don't offend the public. Don't be too controversial. When I asked the editor of a major metropolitan daily why they had endorsed a candidate who merited being denounced rather than endorsed, I was told, "We thought he would win, and we want to work with him." They passed the course in Pandering 101! If a newspaper has an editorial urging the city council or a state legislative committee or a congressional committee to take a specific action, the day after that council or committee votes, the newspaper should have an editorial stating who voted in the public interest, from the newspaper's perspective, and who didn't. Public officials often pay little attention to editorials because they know there will be no follow-through. That's important for a baseball pitcher, a tennis player, and an editorial writer. Editorials need more backbone and muscle.

Campaign Coverage

Coverage of presidential campaigns is not what it should be. In the GOP presidential primary of 1996, the average length of a "sound bite" on network television news was 7.2 seconds. Try saying something significant in 7.2 seconds on any subject! For the first three months of that GOP primary, there were 795 sound bites of less than 10 seconds, 253 of 10 to 19 seconds, 24 of 20 to 29 seconds, and 8 of 30 seconds or more.[16] About half the coverage was on the "horse race," who gained or lost a few points in the latest polls. That is easy picking for a reporter—much simpler than a story on where the candidates stand on international trade. With the exception in the 2000 campaign of Senator John McCain's drumbeat on the issue of campaign finance reform, most people had no idea what the candidates stood for either in 1996 or 2000. Several newspapers should be given credit for their substantial work on the issue of campaign finance reform. These are good stories, perhaps not widely read, but important for the public to know. But generally, the trivial gets attention. When Bob Dole fell off a platform in 1996, it received far more attention than anything he said or did during the rest of the campaign. But a story about falling off a platform is much easier for a reporter than where the two candidates stand on health care or almost any significant issue. The platform story interests the public, and it's inexpensive to do. It's hard to beat a combination of pleasing the public and making more money.

In January 2000, the major networks devoted 30 percent less time to the presidential candidates than in January 1996. In the preseason part of the campaigns, network airtime in 1999 was half the 1995 exposure. And the shift from positive news, in which the candidate explains his or her views on a subject, to stressing negative incidents has been pronounced.

Morton Mintz, the respected but retired *Washington Post* reporter, says that journalists should be raising fundamental questions that candidates are not addressing. That seems obvious, but a combination of candidates excessively shielded from reporters, journalists numbed by the repetitive nature of the standard stump speech of the candidates, and the diminished coverage of campaigns tends to limit these important explorations. However, editorials could address open letters to the candidates, with blunt questions hitting the tough areas too many candidates avoid. Charles Peters of the *Washington Monthly* says part of the problem is "the intellectual shallowness of the average reporter. They're extremely bright people . . . but they don't get into issues deeply."[17]

New York Times reporter Adam Clymer told the American Political Science Association, "There is no question that news organizations with big investments in polls overplay them."[18] When candidates finally get their set speech down, that is repeated endlessly, with minor modifications for whatever may be in the news that day or with comments about a local issue, the habit of making poll fluctuations the big story is somewhat understandable. What the campaign means to Joe Jones and Jane Smith—two among the forty-three million Americans without health care coverage—takes much more work for a reporter. The superficiality of much campaign rhetoric is compounded by the superficiality of media coverage. A serious speech about health care does not fit into a 10-second sound bite.

Readers with good memories may recall that in 1988 I sought the Democratic nomination for president. The hectic schedule of campaigning makes attempts at solid discussion of the issues difficult, particularly when you know that coverage of anything serious will be slim. My staff and I learned that in Iowa or New Hampshire or at any other stop, if we announced that I would bowl a line or do something else that would make a good "visual," we could get coverage and occasionally get in a few words on a serious subject.

An in-depth study of all the media in the 1992 presidential race found only 15.5 percent of the news devoted to policy issues.[19] Al Hunt of the *Wall Street Journal* accurately notes, "Buying air time is often the only way a candidate can get a message out."[20]

Former *Washington Post* reporter Paul Taylor, now the executive director of the Alliance for Better Campaigns, writes:

> The Brits held a national election last month for the bargain price of $60 million. That's 1.5 percent of what we spent on our 2000 campaign. . . . If they can elect their entire Parliament and prime minister for less money than a single deep-pocketed candidate spent to win a single U.S. Senate seat . . . it's worth asking how.
>
> Part of the explanation is that Brits don't allow political ads on television. Instead, like almost all of the world's democracies, they require broadcasters to provide free air time. . . .
>
> The free air time spots were two and a half to five minutes long, and each major party was allotted five during the campaign. They were a bit more substantive than our 30-second spots. . . .
>
> Each of the major parties holds a televised press conference every morning, and the major candidates submit to long, frequent and often combative interviews. . . . In short, there are lots of ways that political information gets delivered on television—all for free, and all meatier than our campaign commercials.[21]

The Alliance for Better Campaigns, with former presidents Jimmy Carter and Gerald Ford, as well as Walter Cronkite, serving as honorary cochairs, is pushing for more and better campaign coverage and for free airtime for major candidates.

If, for example, television and radio stations were required to provide two- to three-minute spots where the candidate had to be on camera or before the microphone, there would be at least a minimal discussion of the issues and fewer negative commercials. In 30-second commercials, slick television productions can make almost anyone look like George Washington. But have the candidate get on that tube or mike for two minutes, and there is much more likely to be genuine discussion of the issues. The unpaid commercials would tend to be more constructive and less negative. The present negative commercials rarely feature the candidates. Instead, they feature someone who looks like John or Jane Average Citizen, stopping in front of a store to tell what a terrible person the opponent is. If we had 30-second commercials of airlines depicting crashes of their competitors' planes, soon a high percentage of the nation would lose confidence in the airlines. That is what is happening to our political process.

A small—perhaps not so small—item of good news is that Hearst-Argyle Television, which owns twenty-four television stations, aired at least five minutes a night of campaign news and candidate discussion for thirty days before the 2002 elections.

Walter Cronkite states: "Broadcasters have been given billions of dollars worth of exclusive licenses, free of charge, to use our scarce public airwaves—but only on condition that they serve the public interest. The best way for this great medium to discharge its responsibility under the law is by providing free air time before elections so that, without having to raise money from special interests, candidates can deliver—and citizens receive—the information needed for our democracy to flourish."[22]

The majority of Americans get their political news from television coverage that is generally shallow. Cronkite says: "That means they're inadequately informed, too poorly informed to exercise their rights in a democracy. You cannot give people enough information on the nightly news."[23] It is even worse than that. More time is consumed on television by campaign commercials than by election news. The public often cannot distinguish between the two, since commercials are often purposely structured to look like news items.

While television stations curtailed their news coverage in the 2000 campaign, spending on political advertising almost doubled over the previous four years. In 1996, the top 75 media markets took in $436 million in advertising, and in 2000, $771 million. This amount "covers ad spending on the 484 stations in the nation's 75 largest markets, but excludes the ad dollar spent on roughly 800 stations in the nation's 135 smaller markets. . . . Some Wall Street analysts estimate the actual political ad revenue total was closer to $1 billion."[24]

Television complicates the civic process also in other ways. In *Bowling Alone,* Robert Putnam points out, "More television watching means less of virtually every form of civic participation and social involvement." Buttressing the observations of Walter Cronkite above, Putnam notes, "Those who *read* the news are more engaged and knowledgeable about the world than those who only *watch* the news" (Putnam's emphasis).[25] Language scholar Frederick Betz writes: "Who reads serious commentary? Even most of those who can read, don't."[26]

However, the television landscape is not all desert. *Sixty Minutes, Nightline, 20/20,* some of the cable shows like that of Brian Williams, and the *Jim Lehrer News Hour* and Charlie Rose on PBS—other programs could be cited—all of them are good but most have smaller audiences than the broadcast network news shows or the local news programs. A particularly important contribution has been made by Brian Lamb and the cable industry with C-SPAN. Again, its audience is small, but those who follow C-SPAN with some regularity—and there are C-SPAN junkies out there—come to understand the issues and the political process much better than most citizens do. Lamb has not received adequate national recognition for his service, as far as I am aware, and he deserves a national honor.

Religion Coverage

Religion hit the news with renewed force after September 11, when Muslim zealots, apparently believing they were doing Allah's bidding, crashed two airliners into the World Trade Center towers in New York City, another into the Pentagon, and a fourth plane into the ground in Pennsylvania, short of its intended target in Washington, D.C. How well-informed are we on the world of religion that motivates so many people?

Only one major television network has had a religion reporter, ABC. But in May 2001, that network followed the rest by dismissing Peggy Wehmeyer, who handled that assignment. The *New York Times* has fifty-seven reporters covering sports, two covering religion. The *Los Angeles Times*, *Time*, *Newsweek*, and other publications have good reporters covering religion—but nationally, there are only a few of them—and too little attention is devoted to the beliefs of much of the rest of the world.

I have traveled a fair amount over the years to many nations, but when militants in Iran grabbed hostages at our U.S. embassy in Teheran in 1979, I started reading about Shiite Muslims and Sunni Muslims. I had a reasonable familiarity with the various branches of Christianity and Judaism, but nothing in my educational background or reading of current events gave me any preparation or understanding of this important chasm in the Muslim world. In part, that probably reflects my own reading habits, but in part, it also reflects our national self-absorption—paying attention almost solely to "our group" in the world of religion.

We know about the struggle within the Southern Baptists for their sense of direction, but we know little more about them. After September 11, we saw a surge of Christian and Jewish leaders reaching out to Muslims within our communities but stumbling awkwardly because they, like Americans in general, are so poorly informed.

One of the results of our citizenry being poorly informed about religious beliefs is that we take twists and turns that are not always healthy. Thomas Jefferson's beliefs as a Deist—Unitarian, in today's terms—became an issue in his first presidential race, when opponents badly distorted his convictions. In 1928 in the Al Smith versus Herbert Hoover contest, Smith's Catholicism became a major issue, as it did in John F. Kennedy's race in 1960. Political reporters found handling faith issues awkward in the Bush-Gore race, and because of the paucity of religion journalists, political reporters had to cover it. When in 1984 the senior George Bush—who never felt comfortable with the religious right and they never felt comfortable with him—said he was a "born again" Christian, not a term Episcopalians ordinarily use, insightful observations by the media were almost nonexistent. In the 2000 campaign, Al Gore said that when he faced difficult decisions, he asked, "What would Jesus do?" When George W. Bush was asked a question about his favorite philosopher, he replied, "Christ, because he changed my heart." As the governor of Texas, Bush proclaimed a "Jesus Day." In one of the presidential debates, he said, "Our nation is chosen by God and commissioned by history to be the model to the world of justice and inclusion and diversity without division."[27] That pleases an American audience, but where were the commentators to puncture that balloon?

The only perceptive observation I read was an editorial in the *Weekly Standard*: "Much of this is not religion, but religiosity; not righteousness, but self-righteousness; not piety, but pietism. . . . The return of religion to public life seems better than the absence only by the smallest of margins."[28] A year after the events of September 11, Patricia Williams wrote in the *Nation*, "I'm worried about the degree to which religious fervor seems to have merged with America's new nationalism."[29]

The danger is that political leaders use religion for political ends. While there is a big distance between what we have seen here and the drumming up of anti-Muslim sentiment in India by a few Hindu political leaders or the anti-Hindu appeal by a few Muslim politicians, we have to be careful not to open the door, even a crack, to those possibilities. Former Canadian prime minister Brian Mulroney told me that the religious pandering that has started to penetrate U.S. elections would cause a strong adverse reaction in Canadian politics. But no reporter from a major newspaper or television network presented us with that information. And that's not likely to change as long as accountants determine policy for the media, because they see no immediate payoff in having reporters on religion who can handle things more deftly.

International Coverage

Shortly before the September 11 terrorist attack, the publisher of *U.S. News and World Report* told a luncheon meeting in Chicago that the magazine would cut back on international news because the public is not interested. The "world" part of the magazine's title would become even smaller.

If this were one isolated incident of reducing international coverage, it would be bad news but not that disturbing. Unfortunately, it is part of a pre–September 11 trend in almost all the media. There's no short-term profit. Former *Christian Century* editor James Wall writes: "We have allowed market forces to control television—and the rest of our modern communications media—to such a degree that the lowest common denominator of interest prevails. A free society rises or falls on the exercise of a collective responsibility. When we fail to respond to the needs and vulnerabilities of our citizens, we revert to the law of the jungle."[30]

When former senator George Mitchell returned from Ireland, after successfully negotiating an internationally acclaimed, but precarious peace agreement between the two factions in Northern Ireland, he made his first public appearance in Washington, D.C. One wire service reporter showed up. If he had been Monica Lewinsky, two hundred reporters would have been present.

Even more disturbing, but almost unknown to the public, a massive genocide occurred in Rwanda, in central Africa, in 1994 when eight hundred thousand to one million people were slaughtered. The United Nations in August 1993 had agreed to "guarantee peace throughout the country."[31] I called General Romeo Dallaire, the Canadian in charge of a small contingent of about two hundred fifty UN troops in Kigali, the capital city. Senator James Jeffords of Vermont joined me in the phone call. General Dallaire told us he could stop the slaughter, then in its infancy, if he could get five thousand to eight thousand troops quickly. Senator Jeffords and I had a letter hand-delivered to the White House that afternoon, urging that a meeting of the UN Security Council be called immediately and that if the United States was not willing to send troops, we should at least provide transportation. I waited several days and received no reply. Then I called the White House and was told, "There isn't a base of public support for doing anything in Africa." That anemic reply was no excuse. The president could have gone on television and explained the situation, and a majority of the American people would have supported the action—and even if they did not, the president could have acted; that's what leadership is about. Sacrificing a little popularity now and then is an essential part of effective leadership. But there is also an element of truth to the White House response. A base of support had not been built by U.S. media paying any attention to that part of the world. General Dallaire then made an appeal to UN headquarters for troops to stop the mass killings. A British writer explains: "It quickly became clear that support for a large mission was nonexistent. . . . Advance messages from the U.S. delegation in particular made it clear that there would be no support for a large mission in Rwanda."[32] (When he refers to a "large mission," that is the five thousand to eight thousand troops.) The United States would not have taken this death-creating stand if the administration had felt there would be media criticism, or even media interest.

In their book analyzing American news delivery, Leonard Downie Jr. and Robert Kaiser write:

> Although Americans are more globally connected than ever, most news media steadily and substantially reduced their coverage of foreign news during the last years of the twentieth century, depriving Americans of the opportunity to follow the world around them. . . . There was no consumer rebellion when the networks cut back on foreign coverage. . . . In a time of broad prosperity and relative tranquility, Americans happily consumed entertainment . . . labeled "news." And they happily bought the products advertisers tried to sell them while they consumed those entertainments.[33]

The two authors interviewed Andrew Lack, then president of NBC News, who told them he had no need for a bureau in Rome, because not a single story had come out of Rome during the seven years of his presidency. "When the Pope dies . . . I'll have those pictures without having to have a Rome reporter." The book's authors note that during the seven years of Lack's leadership at NBC News, the *Los Angeles Times* printed more than 320 articles from Rome.[34]

Another incident reflects our culture:

> James J. Kilpatrick, the conservative syndicated columnist, was speaking to an audience of Third World visitors . . . gathering to discuss the American news media. An African stood up to ask a question.
>
> "Why is it that American journalists don't care about my country?"
>
> "What country do you come from, sir?" Kilpatrick asked.
>
> "Uganda."
>
> "Why the hell should I care about Uganda?"
>
> A collective sucking-in breath; stunned silence. The pugnacious columnist went on to explain. Americans, he said,

> are preoccupied with their immediate community and with local issues like taxes, the school system and neighborhood crime. They cannot relate to events in Uganda or any other remote country.[35]

The blunt-spoken but likable Kilpatrick is more sensitive than this story suggests, but it is illustrative of the thinking of large numbers of Americans who have no great desire to be awakened from a peaceful, slumbering indifference to the rest of the world. Television, radio, magazines, and newspapers do too little to awaken us. Terrorists have bestirred us temporarily. Among newspapers, the *New York Times* is the major exception on general international news, and the *Wall Street Journal* on international economic news. Foreign coverage by the *Los Angeles Times, Chicago Tribune, Washington Post, Miami Herald* and a few other newspapers remains good, but many newspapers and magazines that once proudly gave us much information about the rest of the world do not now.

One other publisher should be cited. In 2000, Edward Seaton of the *Manhattan (Kansas) Mercury* became president of the American Society of Newspaper Editors. To the amazement of many, this publisher from the middle of Kansas started pushing for greater coverage of, and sensitivity to, international news. What many did not know is that he had served as a Fulbright scholar in Ecuador, and he and his wife both speak Spanish. His newspaper stresses local connections to international events, made easier because of the presence of Kansas State University in Manhattan. His staff knows of his concerns, and everything from the editorials to the regular columns reflect his interest in what happens beyond our borders. The newspaper has a page titled *Focus* that carries news items from the state, the nation, and the world, and about half the news there is international. To his local critics, Seaton points out that Kansas sells more per capita in international trade than any other state. It is clear he wants his readers to feel a part of the world scene; he has a sense of mission.

In commenting on newspaper coverage of the September 11 terrorist attack, Seaton told *Columbia Journalism Review:* "We did not examine the country's anti-terrorism efforts adequately, our intelligence capabilities, our immigration policies, or the reasons for anti-Americanism. While we can debate whether this failure played a role in our national lack of preparedness, there is no question that we failed our readers." He added, "Local [news] has to be the priority, but editors fail readers if they don't expand the readers' horizons."[36] Other publishers and editors should follow Seaton's example. The Associated Press and other wire services do carry international news items, but too rarely are they picked up. It costs a newspaper (or radio or television station) not one thin dime to instruct key personnel to use more international coverage.

At the World Economic Forum held in early 2002 in New York City, Zaki Laidi of the French Center for International Research told the gathering that there is resentment in many nations toward the United States, "which so influences the world while its own population has no interest in the world."[37] Why is there so little interest on the part of U.S. citizens? One of the reasons—not the only one—is the lack of attention to the international scene by the media, except for crisis events.

It is not only the lack of coverage that is a problem but also the quality of the coverage. Henry Kissinger observes: "Ubiquitous and clamorous media are transforming foreign policy into a subdivision of public entertainment. The intense competition for ratings produces an obsession with the crisis of the moment, generally presented as a morality play between good and evil having a specific outcome and rarely in terms of the long-range challenges of history. As soon as the flurry of excitement has subsided, the media move on to new sensations."[38]

A study of international coverage by the Freedom Forum and the American Society of Newspaper Editors noted another flaw, based in large part on the thin base of knowledge of international matters by American reporters: "Foreign coverage is too dominated by official U.S. policy interests."[39]

With the exception of CNN, television's pre–September 11 international coverage can be charitably described as woefully inadequate. *Miserable* is a more accurate description. And CNN is now tilting more toward entertainment. In 1997, veteran foreign correspondent Garrick Utley wrote an article for *Foreign Affairs* appropriately titled "The Shrinking of Foreign News."[40] He quoted from the *Tyndall Report* that network nightly international news coverage declined from 3,733 minutes in 1989 to 1,175 in 1996 at NBC, the last in the rankings before Fox came on the scene. Utley also reported that "in the half-hour format, [international] reports initially ran a minimum of two and a half minutes and often three to five minutes, compared with one and a half minutes or even less today." Until the September 11 tragedy, the decline continued. In 2001—before September 11—CBS had nine foreign correspondents, NBC eight, ABC seven, and Fox six. Most of these now are based in London and are flown to the place of news, resulting in—at best—superficial coverage of an issue. The chance to live and learn in depth about another nation and another culture is denied them. ABC calls its evening newscast *World News Tonight*, but there is little "world" news on it. CNN, in the process of reducing its staff by four hundred when September 11 occurred, now has fifty-five correspondents stationed abroad.

While the viewership and readership surveys reflect a lack of interest in international news, Michael Parks, former editor of the *Los Angeles Times*, notes that news broadcasts and publications that cover international events do well: "NPR's Morning Edition and All Things Considered have a growing audience; the *Economist's* U.S. circulation increased 11 percent in the last year, and 66 percent over the last decade; the BBC's international radio and television newscasts are carried by an increasing number of public broadcasting stations."[41] Are these numbers reflective of a deepening interest in what happens in other nations by the bulk of our population? Regrettably, that is not the case. Because of terrorist action, there is a temporary surge, but every indication is that we are returning to our habits of international slumbering.

At a time when the United States is singular in its huge ability to influence the world, our people are less and less interested in matters beyond our borders, and our leaders reflect that. The media does far too little to break that irresponsible habit of indifference. Pandering to our popular and current tastes helps short-term profits and hurts the nation—and in the long run hurts the media. Marvin Kalb observes that the news business has changed "from one proudly tied to public service to one unashamedly linked to the pursuit of public titillation and maximum profit."[42]

Even small media outlets with few resources can improve their reporting of foreign news and serve the public better. It may be something as simple as an interview with an international student at a nearby college, or a story about a foreign diplomat or a missionary visiting a community. Like the international student, the political refugee in a community can give media outlets the opportunity for an interview that may help to sensitize readers, viewers, and listeners to a world beyond their community and our nation.

The *St. Louis Post-Dispatch* occasionally sends reporters to another nation or region for a few days or a few weeks to report on an issue—not as good as having a bureau abroad but better than nothing. Freedom Forum, in cooperation with the American Society of Newspaper Editors, has published a how-to booklet, *Bringing the World Home,* with ideas for international coverage. In it, Seymour Topping of the *New York Times* suggests asking people in a newsroom, including copy editors, to pay particular attention to some assigned region or nation; a small thing, but it helps.

Even some of the smallest newspapers, radio stations, television outlets, and magazines could, once every two years, send a reporter to some developing nation for two weeks to report back to the local people. Would that sometimes result in superficial reporting? Yes, but superficial reporting is generally better than no reporting. Doing this is also a way to say to the public that this broadcast or publishing medium is a class operation, that it is engaged in more than making a fast buck.

Television Violence

More than a decade ago, I accidentally stumbled onto the issue of violence on entertainment television. Staying overnight at a motel in LaSalle County, Illinois, I turned on my television set, and suddenly in front of me, I saw someone being sawed in half by a chain saw. I was old enough to know it wasn't real, but it bothered me that night, and I wondered what would happen to a ten-year-old who watched it. I called my staff and told them I was sure that someone has done research on this. I wanted to know about it.

The answer came back that there is research, and it shows harm is done. Several universities had done studies; the National Institute of Mental Health and the American Academy of Pediatrics issued warnings about violence on entertainment television.

I invited representatives of the television industry to my office and told them that we have a problem. I explained that both as a former journalist and as a long-time member of the American Civil Liberties Union, I do not want government censorship, but I thought they should establish standards on a voluntary basis. The vice president of one network told me that they had research that showed that entertainment violence does no harm. I told him that he reminded me of the Tobacco Institute people who come into my office to tell me that their research shows that cigarettes do no harm. "The question is not whether harm is done," I told them. "The question is what you will do about it."

The industry representatives said they could not agree on standards because that would violate antitrust laws. So I introduced legislation—which they opposed—to make an exemption in the antitrust laws for this one purpose only. It passed, and the senior President George Bush signed it into law.[43] The industry slowly moved into adopting standards, the broadcast and cable divisions adopting somewhat different standards, both of them anemic. Particularly playing responsible roles in broadcasting were Howard Stringer, then president of CBS News and a key CBS executive, and Tom Murphy, then chief executive officer of ABC. Broadcast television did reduce the violence, though this happened before the emergence of Fox Television, which in its eagerness to pick up viewers has stretched the limits not only of violence but also of sex and language. Even Fox went too far in a program "which bound contestants in a chair and exposed them to either subzero temperatures or to flames that raised the temperature past 150 degrees Fahrenheit . . . subjecting people to what appeared to be torture for the entertainment of television viewers."[44] After showing the second episode, Fox dropped the program—probably not because of the criticism it received but because the audience declined from the first episode, which had approximately 10 million viewers, down to 5.6 million for the second. Television sometimes goes too far in appealing to our cruder instincts. Broadcast television generally has been better than cable, though Ted Turner and the late Tony Cox tried to move cable in a constructive direction. Public television is clearly the most responsible of the major outlets, both in its adult programming and in its children's programming.

I have never suggested there should be no violence on television. But it should not be glorified. If someone produces a film about the Civil War, it will have violence, but it should be realistic, and it should be grim. Nor have I suggested that the news be violence-free. When the evening news pictures someone killed in Bosnia or the Middle East or Chicago, it is realistic, with people weeping and agony on the faces of the survivors. My son,

Martin Simon, is a news photographer who won a national award for his picture of the first burial of a serviceman in Arlington National Cemetery after Desert Storm. *Life* magazine published a book that included this picture, and it quotes my son: "As soon as I saw the younger boy in his father's flight jacket, and the mother in red, I knew it was going to be an emotional scene. I'd seen so many glorified images of Desert Storm, I wanted to show another side."[45] That "other side" of violence is rarely portrayed during entertainment television time.

One not-so-incidental result of television violence: Studies show that adults who spend above average time watching television have a greatly exaggerated estimate of the crime rates in their communities, one of the factors in the pressure on policy makers to pass lengthy mandatory minimum sentences that serve no one's best interests.

At my request, both broadcast and cable television authorized three-year studies of television violence, probably calculating that the results would make the industry look good. Five universities—UCLA, the University of California at Santa Barbara, the University of North Carolina at Chapel Hill, the University of Wisconsin at Madison, and the University of Texas at Austin—conducted the studies. Among their conclusions: 73 percent of the depiction of violence on entertainment television shows no immediate adverse effect on the person committing the violence, and only 4 percent of the portrayed mayhem has an antiviolence theme. Children and emotionally immature adults learn the obvious lesson: violence pays. We have the most violent television of any nation, with the possible exception of Japan, and there the violence is ordinarily perpetrated by "the bad guys," while on American television the violence is usually committed by "the good guys," the people with whom we—and particularly children—identify. One well-known children's program is produced in two versions: the violent version for the United States, and the nonviolent version for the rest of the world. When asked about this by the *Christian Science Monitor*, the producer said they had received no complaints about the violence in the United States, and people seemed to like it, but they cannot sell the violent version in other nations.

An advisory council put together by the cable industry included representatives of the Directors Guild, Producers Guild, and the American Federation of Television and Radio Artists. The council noted that "anti-violence messages are scarce on [entertainment] television."[46] Equally disturbing, the report shows there is more violence in children's programs than in shows designed for adults and that "children's programming is the least likely to depict the long-term negative consequences of violence, and the most likely to depict unrealistically low levels of harm."[47] A twenty-two-year study by the University of Michigan followed 875 boys and girls from age eight until age thirty and concluded "that those who watched more violent television as children are more likely as adults to commit serious crimes and to use violence to punish their own children."[48] Former FCC chairman Newton Minow said, "In 1961 I worried that children would not benefit much from television, but in 1991 I worry that my children will actually be harmed by it."[49]

In December 2000, the National Commission for the Prevention of Youth Violence, composed of some of the nation's leaders in medicine, nursing, and public health, listed as a priority reducing our exposure to media violence. The report comments: "Children and youth are greatly influenced by what they hear and see in movies, television, the Internet, video games, and music. Extensive evidence documents the strong, pervasive, and deleterious effects of media violence on children. The media industry must be responsive to these scientific data."[50]

Professor John P. Murray of Kansas State University joined with other researchers to study the impact on a child's brain of watching television violence. The results are measurable and disturbing, causing both short-term and long-term harm.[51] Long before the advent of television, Plato wrote in the *Republic*: "Shall we just carelessly allow children to hear any casual tales which may be devised by casual persons, and to receive into their minds ideas for the most part the very opposite of those which we should wish them to have when they are grown up? We cannot. . . . Anything received into the mind at that age is likely to become indelible and unalterable; and therefore it is most important that the tales which the young first hear should be models of virtuous thoughts."[52]

The Institute for Mental Health Initiatives reported:

> What is a healthy experience that confirms one viewer's abhorrence of violent solutions can be dangerously overstimulating for another, particularly for children and teenagers. . . . Children, teenagers, and adults whose life experiences and temperament have combined to limit their capacity to delay action or manage anger and fear are candidates for violent behavior. They may merge with the characters they see, losing the boundary between the characters and themselves. . . . Someone who is already angry and/or aroused by drugs [or] alcohol . . . is more likely to be pushed over the edge by viewing violent portrayals.[53]

Isolated incidents abound. In the state of Washington, after two teenagers were arrested for several brutal murders, their friends commented that the two had been influenced by a television show they saw that "concerns immortals whose powers are enhanced when they cut off people's heads."[54] Isolated incidents are not proof, but when there are so many of them, and they are backed by substantial studies, we should learn something.

I also believe that we have a problem with the portrayal of sex and the use of coarse language, but there have been no solid studies on these as there have been about television violence. When research shows that only 9 percent of the acts of sex that are implied but not shown on television are between married couples, my strong sense is that we are harming the nation. When I hear language vulgarities, I know that children pick them up, and it cheapens our communication. But again, these concerns based on sex and language issues are instinct, not backed by solid studies, as in the case of entertainment violence portrayal.

Film and television critic Stanley Crouch is quoted in *Time* magazine: "When questions are raised about . . . certain material, the industry's executives tell us it has no influence." Television executives have told me the same thing. They say that a 30-second commercial can sell a Chevrolet or a bar of soap, but 25 minutes of glorification of violence has no influence on children. Crouch continues: "The Third Reich proved beyond all reasonable doubt what the constant pumping of hate-filled images and inflammatory statements can do to a culture. I do not believe censorship is the answer. . . . We need [a] sense of responsibility."[55] Former Secretary of Education William Bennett calls some of the leaders of the television and movie industry "morally disabled."[56] He may be correct, but whatever the reason for the choices they make when producing a movie or developing a programming list, we need them to act in a responsible way, paying close attention to the content of programs and considering how that content may impact viewers.

A 1994 poll by MTV of sixteen- to twenty-nine-year-olds showed that 40 percent believed that "nonviolence does not work any more." It would be wrong to say that they acquired that attitude only through watching television, but television has to share the blame for the attitudes of this age group that watches so much TV.

Entertainment in its crudest form reaches us in World Wrestling Federation matches—and they attract huge audiences. There are those who believe that these "fights" are so coarse and so obviously phony that they have less of a bad influence than the more sophisticated depictions of violence. I don't know who is right about this. They're both bad.

The Center for Media and Public Affairs did a study of 573 programs during the 1998–99 season. They found:

- [Of the] 8,350 scenes of violence, 4,204 of those involved murder, rape, kidnapping, or assault with a weapon.
- Most acts of violence were not presented as causing either physical or emotional harm. Bullets frequently miss their mark, heroes bounce back from beatings without a scratch, and few victims of violence are emotionally traumatized. Violence was often carried out by good guys, who acted out of laudable motives. Scripts almost never carried explicit criticism of the use of violence.
- Television violence is heavily concentrated in programming aimed at young people.

The report also notes: "The American Psychological Association estimates that the average twelve-year-old has seen 8,000 murders and 100,000 acts of violence on network television. Over three decades of research, summarized in reports by the National Institute of Mental Health, have documented the harmful effects of such violent entertainment. . . . In response to such findings, the American Medical Association passed a resolution declaring that television violence 'threatens the health and welfare of young Americans.' "[57]

A *New York Times* article of March 29, 2002, has this significant news:

> Teenagers and young adults who watched more than one hour of television daily were more likely to commit violent crimes and engage in other forms of aggressive behavior later, according to a new report.
>
> An association between television violence and aggression has been well established by studies over the last four decades. But most research has focused on the television viewing habits of children. The new study, published today in the journal Science, searched for a relationship between television watching and aggression in an older group.

The investigators, led by Dr. Jeffrey G. Johnson of Columbia University and the New York State Psychiatric Institute, followed children in 707 families in two counties in northern New York State for 17 years. They reported that adolescents and young adults who watched television for more than seven hours a week had an increased likelihood of committing an aggressive act in later years. . . .

This was the first long-term study to link violent behavior and television watching by teenagers and young adults. The study which is continuing, began when the children were 1 to 10 years old. . . .

In their analysis, the investigators used a statistical model to take into account other factors, like poverty, childhood neglect and the presence of a psychiatric disorder, that have been linked to violence. Still, they said, there was a link between television watching and aggressive or violent behavior in boys, but nothing significant in girls. . . .

Now, said Dr. Leonard Eron, a psychology professor at the University of Michigan and a pioneer in the study of television's effects on behavior, "this shows that adolescents and young adults are also affected."

That, he added, was not necessarily expected. "My own feeling was that children are very impressionable and that this is the way they learn by watching others," Dr. Eron said. "I did not know it would affect people later in their development."

Dr. Dale Kunkel, a professor of communications at the University of California at Santa Barbara, said the new study "is another rock on an already huge pile of evidence documenting the relationship between media violence and real-world violence and aggression."

Dr. Johnson said the results had important implications for society.

"By decreasing exposure to media violence, we may be able to prevent millions of Americans from being raped and murdered," he said in an interview this week.[58]

"Millions" is an exaggerated figure, but the study cited confirms again that the pursuit of dollars—regardless of the costs to society—by television executives is a bloodthirsty endeavor.

No informed person would suggest that television entertainment violence is the sole cause of crime in our society. But no one who looks seriously at the research can come away without an awareness that it is one of the causes, along with the lack of sensible gun control laws, inattention to poverty and joblessness, and other factors. However, putting the blame on the public rather than accepting responsibility, like many in the newspaper industry have done, television executives often cite the public's desires as a defense for the programming they choose to air. They must learn to practice self-restraint.

A free system works best when people exercise self-restraint. When Richard Nixon lost to John F. Kennedy in a tight race, Nixon could have called people into the street to protest, but instead he congratulated Kennedy. A few years later, Hubert Humphrey lost a tight race to Richard Nixon, and again the same thing happened. There would have been nothing illegal about Nixon's and Humphrey's asking for massive street protests, but they did not. Al Gore lost to George W. Bush in the tightest of races when a 5–4 decision in the U.S. Supreme Court went against him. Gore made the finest speech of his campaign, saying, "I disagree with the decision, but I accept it."

Yes, our economy is based in large part on the private enterprise system, where people are free to make money so long as they operate within the law, but if self-restraint is not exercised, then ultimately the law will change. Both the public and lawmakers understand that there are excesses in television. They want restraint by the industry. I do not want government censorship, but I have learned in four decades of lawmaking that most legislators do not have great sensitivity to the First Amendment. If it's a choice of following public opinion or safeguarding the First Amendment, the constitution loses.

At a gathering of leaders in television and movies as well as academic specialists at the University of California at Santa Barbara on April 11, 1997, I concluded my remarks with these observations:

> I am old enough to remember the movies of World War II and how they aided the nation in a time of crisis. We are once again in a time of national crisis but of less dramatic proportions. Can public officials act responsibly, reducing poverty and crime and violence without reducing freedom? The answer is that they can. What we do not know is if they will. On that decision rests part of the future of the nation. Can television and movie directors and executives act responsibly, reducing the glamorization of violence while preserving artistic freedom? The answer is they can. What we do not know is if they will. On that decision rests part of the future of the nation.

Mergers—and More Mergers

Just as many of the distortions in the media are caused by the addiction to dollars, so that same appetite for money has caused an unhealthy merger trend in the media and a resultant diminution of quality.

New York Times columnist William Safire put it simply and correctly: "Concentration of power over what we see in the news is a danger to democracy."[59] In 1948, the distinguished Harvard scholar Zachariah Chafee Jr. wrote, "The sovereign press for the most part acknowledges accountability to no one except its owners and publishers."[60] That had its dangers in 1948, but more than half a century later, the number of media owners has shriveled dramatically, with fewer and fewer people controlling what we read and see and hear. Of the fifteen hundred daily newspapers in the nation, more than twelve hundred are now owned by chains.

Those chains are following market research that shows that the public likes shorter stories, more color, more entertainment. But veteran newsmen Leonard Downie Jr. and Robert Kaiser note in their book, "No newspaper has soared in popularity as a result of such changes."[61] Gene Roberts, former managing editor of the *New York Times*, observes of the U.S. newspaper scene: "When we started cutting back on substance, we put serious, devoted readers at risk by becoming less essential to them. . . . We are imperiling newspapers in the name of saving them."[62] But at least temporarily, they are showing greater profits.

Mergers of newspapers, so that most cities now have only one major newspaper, are not good for the nation, but federal government action to stop or slow that trend can only be marginal. We could charge higher second-class postage rates for any entity owning more than five newspapers, urge the Anti-Trust Division of the Department of Justice to look at acquisitions and mergers carefully, and charge a higher corporate income tax rate for any corporation owning more than ten newspapers—none of these three would be likely to pass—but the role in this field for the federal government is limited. Where corporations own both newspapers and television stations and radio outlets, the federal government could act, but that is becoming less and less likely.

Radio illustrates our problem. Until the passage of the Telecommunications Act of 1996, the Federal Communications Commission limited ownership by one entity to not more than twenty AM stations and twenty FM stations, and not more than one of each in a market. The Telecommunications Act of 1996—and I am proud to have cast one of eighteen votes against it in the Senate—took the lid off. At that point, the Infinity Corporation owned twenty-seven stations and CBS twenty-six. I offered an amendment to place caps of fifty AM stations and fifty FM stations by one owner. I would have preferred keeping the old twenty/twenty rule, but we then faced the total lifting of caps, so I attempted at least a little restraint. My amendment lost 64–34, but I am listing the names of the 33 brave senators who voted with me.[63]

Daniel Akaka	Russell Feingold	Joseph Lieberman
Joseph Biden Jr.	Dianne Feinstein	Barbara Mikulski
Jeff Bingaman	Tom Harkin	Patrick Moynihan
Barbara Boxer	Jesse Helms	Patty Murray
Bill Bradley	Bennett Johnston	Claiborne Pell
Dale Bumpers	Edward Kennedy	David Pryor
Robert Byrd	John Kerry	Harry Reid
Kent Conrad	Bob Kerrey	Charles Robb
Mike DeWine	Frank Lautenberg	John Rockefeller IV
Christopher Dodd	Patrick Leahy	Paul Sarbanes
Byron Dorgan	Carl Levin	Paul Wellstone

What has happened since then? Within weeks of the passage of the bill, billions of dollars were spent acquiring radio stations. During the first year of the act, media moguls spent $13.6 billion to acquire 2,045 radio stations, or roughly one-fifth of the radio outlets in the nation, most of them in metropolitan areas with large audiences. Headlines like this spread across the nation: "CBS Radio to Get Five More Stations in St. Louis Market."[64] The deal meant that CBS would have 60 percent of the listeners and advertising in St. Louis. In Cincinnati, Jacor Communications bought eight stations. Within three years, over half the radio stations in the nation had been sold, and one corporation owned 830 stations. The numbers keep rising. One report noted with alarm that two radio giants "now control over a third of all radio advertising revenue nationally, and up to 90 percent in some markets."[65] FCC Commissioner Susan Ness called the consolidation of the radio industry "breathtaking."[66] Good local coverage of the news on community radio stations is now only a memory for many Americans. When we have evening speakers at Southern Illinois University, such as former New York City mayor David Dinkins or former Canadian prime minister Brian Mulroney, there is no local commercial radio coverage. Consolidation of ownership has resulted in diminished coverage and no evening reporters. In many instances, along with poorer coverage has come advertising rate increases of 20 percent to 50 percent, as consolidation of ownership reduced competition. One study concludes, "Costs are down while profits and advertising revenues for radio have risen significantly as a result of deregulation."[67]

The former CEO of one of the largest stations in the nation wrote to me: "You and those in the Senate who joined you in behalf of a cap on radio ownership were eminently sound. Your words of warning should have been heeded. . . . What has transpired is against the public interest and represents, in my opinion, an act of irresponsibility on the part of Congress."[68] Proponents of the act promised more competition and better news coverage for all Americans. The result has been less competition and poorer quality coverage, not because of the ability of the reporters but because fewer reporters are covering events.

The business types who manage the corporate entities look for higher profits and quicker profits, and more reporters would mean fewer immediate profits. A financial analyst for Merrill Lynch, commenting favorably on Knight Ridder stock, noted that the company's "historic culture has been one of producing Pulitzer Prizes instead of profits, and while we think that culture is hard to change, it does seem to be happening."[69] In a panel moderated by Walter Cronkite, Pulitzer Prize–winner Alex Jones, a former *New York Times* reporter and coauthor of a book about that newspaper, observed accurately: "My sense is that the wisdom in the newspaper industry these days is that we want to protect our profit margin; that's the top priority. And that's being done by a reduction of news."[70] Coverage of the then-pending telecommunications proposal tilted heavily on the favorable side, understandably. Few reporters understood that it would result in concentration of media power, and those who did know generally did not want to "bite the hand that feeds them." Only 16 percent of the stories even mentioned media concentration, and only 4 percent of broadcast evening news was devoted to this lucrative part of the bill.[71] Calling attention to this aspect of the proposal would not be helpful in advancing a person's career. This is the same problem the issue of television entertainment violence faced. Covering the surgeon general's warnings about cigarettes received big coverage; the financial stakes for the media were small. When the surgeon general warned about television violence, it received much less attention. When the Telecommunications Act passed, an article in the *Media Studies Journal*—read by a small audience—noted that the act "has been hailed as the harbinger of a new era of expanded competition. . . . Although it is intended to unbridle the free forces of the market, it may well end up accelerating the concentration of media power."[72] I read with mixed feeling that the *Chicago Tribune* purchased the Times-Mirror Corporation, publisher of the *Los Angeles Times*. The *Tribune* today is a quality newspaper, and the present leadership will see to it that the *Los Angeles Times*—one of the nation's best—continues to provide excellent coverage. But what does the acquisition mean in the years to come, when the *Tribune*'s leadership changes? What are the implications for radio and television, where both corporations have substantial holdings? And this was not a move made out of desperation. The *Tribune* made a 29.9 percent profit in 1999, before acquiring the *Times-Mirror*, "the highest [profit margin] of any [major] newspaper company."[73] But the *Times-Mirror* itself made an 18.2 percent profit, also a good return if not as impressive as the *Tribune*'s and certainly not an indication of economic collapse that would force a sale or merger.

Cutting back on the number of reporters is not a public-interest way to add to those profits. The studies by the Project for Excellence in Journalism at Columbia University show that "the larger the staff, the higher the news quality scores" in the television stations across the nation that they studied.[74] They also learned that adding a helicopter did not improve either quality ratings or viewership. Beyond that, the studies show both good news and bad news.

The good news is that the stations that provide quality coverage generally had the biggest audiences. The Columbia University study stressed three points:

- At stations rising in ratings, 37 percent of stories were a minute or longer. At stations falling in ratings, the figure was 24 percent.
- At stations rising in ratings, just 39 percent of stories were 30 seconds or shorter. At stations falling in ratings, 55 percent were.
- Stations losing ratings aired almost twice as many super-short stories, less than 20 seconds long.[75]

The best stations, in quality and audience, not only aired longer and better-developed stories but provided less crime coverage and showed more initiative in going after stories. The bad news is that the stations that provided "tabloid news," the most sensational but poorest quality news, also thrived.

Another not-good-news item is that Carol Marin, coanchor of WMAQ-NBC News in Chicago and widely recognized for her courage and thoughtfulness as well as ability, left the station in protest when it announced that Jerry Springer, host of one of television's least cerebral programs, would do commentary on their newscasts. Nielsen ratings showed the NBC outlet running second among the five major commercial newscasts in Chicago—making a profit, but the owners wanted it to be number one and make more money. After a lull, rival station WBBM-CBS announced that Carol Marin would anchor their 10 o'clock evening news, with every indication that it would be a thoughtful product, reflecting the stature of Carol Marin. After nine months, WBBM dropped the experiment. Many observers believe that if they had sustained the program and promoted it more, their ratings would have gradually escalated. But with the revolving-door management at the station, those in charge wanted quick results. That didn't materialize.

If you believe that the mergers, cutbacks in staff, and centralization of ownership have been bad in the past, every indication is that the worst is still to come. When President George W. Bush's new chair of the Federal Communications Commission, Michael Powell, testified before a Senate committee, he indicated he wanted to abrogate some of the few remaining FCC restrictions on consolidation of media ownership. Senator Ron Wyden of Oregon told him, "On your watch we could have the most radical consolidation of media ownership in our history."[76] Powell responded that he places "reliance on deregulation and markets" to determine the future of the media field.

Outside of reduced quality because of staff reductions, has the concentration of ownership resulted in harm? It cannot be measured yet. Yes, we know that when any major metropolitan area has only one newspaper to advocate or oppose causes, that lack of alternative viewpoints weakens the community. When General Electric owns NBC, it is unlikely that stories unfavorable to GE will receive much attention at NBC. However, up to this point, those types of abuses have been rare. When the CBS station in St. Louis refused to air a commercial by Handgun Control Inc., attacking presidential candidate George W. Bush's record on guns, it turned out that the corporation that owns the station, Belo, based in Dallas, Texas, has as its chief executive officer a friend of the then-governor of Texas. Pure coincidence? I don't know, but many believe it is not coincidental. Whether in this case corporate muscle was used to stop the ad, there is no question that more and more of that type of corporate power will be used and abused. Fewer and fewer people are determining what is in our news, and more and more of those decisions are made by people who are looking for quick profits rather than by those who are steeped in the traditions of reporting news. Long-term, quality news coverage pays off. But to business executives who want to look better and better in each quarterly report, the simpler way is to reduce staff and to pander to whatever will satisfy the hunger of a large audience.

In defense of mergers, many argue that we now have more choice than ever with cable television channels and the Internet. It is true that we can watch C-SPAN or the History Channel and other outlets, but the eight-hundred-pound gorillas in the media still dominate, and fewer and fewer people control them. Blunt-speaking Ted Turner, recently with Time Warner, gave us CNN and enriched our culture by doing that, but he admits, "We have just a few people controlling all the cable companies in this country."[77] As to the Internet, University of Illinois media scholar Robert McChesney concludes, "If anything, the Internet is spurring more concentration in media ownership."[78]

In the film industry, six firms now bring in more than 90 percent of theater income in the United States. And book publishing is becoming more and more concentrated.

All in all, not a pretty picture.

Defendants of the new status tell us the same thing is happening in the automobile industry, with the airlines, in banking, and in almost every field. That is true, and it is not good. Theodore Roosevelt would be preaching to us about these evils. But car manufacturers do not control ideas. When we shrink the access to news and opinions, we do much more harm to our free system than from the concentration of resources in any other field.

3

Pandering in Religion

Religion is doing; a man does not merely *think* his religion or feel it, he "lives" his religion as much as he is able, otherwise it is not religion but fantasy or philosophy.

—George Gurdjieff, Greek-Armenian religious teacher

Religion That Comforts but Does Not Challenge

RELIGION CAN BE a powerful force for harm or a powerful force for healing. Those who crashed two airliners into the World Trade Center on September 11 did so with a belief that they were serving the cause of Allah. In the Middle East, the bitterness between the Israelis and the Palestinians has religious roots, which have been exploited for political purposes. When President Bill Clinton made his first visit to Northern Ireland and spoke at a factory near Belfast, journalists noted that the industry had separate employee entrances for Catholics and Protestants. The Thirty Years War in Europe decimated about one-fourth of the population, largely in the name of religion. Slaughter in the name of faith is a tragic part of history.* As one example, when Charles V, the king of France and other parts of Europe, sent his troops to Tunis to free ten thousand Christians a Muslim leader had enslaved there, he not only freed the slaves but "rewarded his unpaid troops by letting them loot the city and massacre the Moslem population."[1] The slaying of six million Jews by Adolf Hitler was made possible, in part, by Catholic and Lutheran anti-Semitism.

Terrible as all these examples are, perhaps the greater sin by faith leaders has been—and is—an unwillingness to do the unpopular; a tendency to comfort and pander to those who attend religious functions regularly but not to disturb them by building bridges to other faiths or by helping the most miserable in our society and our world in concrete ways.

John and Charles Wesley—prime movers in England's much earlier abandonment of slavery than in the United States—had great influence in that country. The Methodists then numbered only 79,000 in all of England, and most were poor. The Wesleys appeared to be minor irritants to the established Church of

*I use terms like *faith* and *congregation* that are not used by all religions, but they are widely understood.

England and to the large but less numerous membership of the Roman Catholic church. The two brothers applied their Christianity to concrete social needs, aiding their nation as well as meeting the individual spiritual longings of their membership—and Methodism grew and prospered. The search for social justice is still a part of Methodism's mission, but the much more prosperous religious membership today has much less influence per capita than in the days of the Wesleys. Why?

A Methodist friend responded to my question: "Methodists, like Lutherans and every other church group, have become fat and comfortable and wealthy and aloof from the problems of people like those to whom the Wesleys preached." What he said about the Methodists applies to most religious bodies. Although journalist James Fallows did not have the religious community targeted when he wrote the following, it applies: "The way a rich nation thinks about its poor will always be convoluted. The richer people become in general, the easier it theoretically becomes for them to share with people who are left out. But the richer people become, the less they naturally stay in touch with realities of life on the bottom, and the more they naturally prefer to be excited about their own prospects rather than concerned about someone else's."[2]

Theologian Reinhold Niebuhr commented decades ago, "The extreme individualism of middle-class religion in the past two centuries has narrowed the religious vision to the individual life, and made personal immortality and perfection the sole goal of religious striving."[3] We too often isolate ourselves from the welfare of the community and from needy individuals within our communities.

Until my father died, I frowned upon wakes, in large part because I often found them awkward, not knowing what to say to survivors and not being comfortable in joining those who seemed to be enjoying themselves too much following someone's death. After my father died, we held the traditional wake at the funeral home in the small community near the Lutheran church where he served as pastor. What impressed me most were people who, although looking a little uncomfortable wearing their best clothes, wanted to share with me how my father had helped them when they faced serious economic problems, or about his volunteering every Thursday morning to go to a school for the mentally retarded and do menial work there. I suddenly realized that my father's best sermons were not those he offered from the pulpit but what he did and how he benefited others, helping to change their lives for the better. That is true for almost all of us of whatever faith, whether we are in the clergy or the laity.

To what extent are today's religious communities social clubs rather than agents of change? I do not suggest that any group should abandon or soften their basic theological beliefs. But they must ask themselves: How do we apply this belief to our lives? How do these beliefs motivate us to act? What should we be doing? It is fine to say that we are meeting the individual spiritual needs of members, but we should build on that base. Many people look for a religious home that approves their comfortable way of life. Too often, that desire is catered to, while any message of concern for the poor and miserable that most religions profess is muted. The closest many local religious assemblies come to challenging adherents is remodeling a church, synagogue, or mosque or building a new one, which is often the right thing to do, but it is sometimes a monument to ourselves and an excuse to bypass greater responsibilities that we should be shouldering. Christians even have a term for the church leader who concentrates on what happens within a church building—baptisms, liturgy, weddings, funerals—and also on stained glass windows, good benches, and the physical accoutrements of the structure but who tends to neglect visiting the sick in the parish and other duties that congregations have come to expect. Such a person is called "a sanctuary pastor," not a phrase of praise. I know of no phrase that describes the clerical leader who fails to reach beyond his or her flock to the poor and desperate, but religious leaders of that type abound.

Early in my life, I helped my local church build a new house of worship. My recollection is that it cost $196,000, then a sizable sum for our small congregation. After it was completed and we had wiped out the debt, if I had gone to the next congregational meeting and suggested that we raise $196,000 to feed hungry people, I know what the response would have been. It is probably a reflection on my lack of faith and zeal and courage that I did not propose it. (If I appear to be picking on Lutherans, it is only because I am one, but with the exception of a few small religious bodies, the criticism I make of Lutherans applies to the entire diversity of religious groups.) The test of faith suggested to Christians by Jesus in Matthew 25 is not whether we built a new church edifice, but what we have done to "help the least of these," the poor, the thirsty, the naked, the hungry, the outcast, the sick, and those in prison.

Newsweek reports that "the median amount spent per congregation on direct assistance to the needy is $1,500 a year; overall social programs attract an average of less than 3 percent of a congregation's annual budget."[4] Yet a frequent and overwhelming command in what Christians call the Old and New Testaments is to take care of the poor. Muslims cite passage after passage from the Qur'an calling for aid to those in great need. Clearly, we are not meeting our obligations in these areas.

A basic document for Jews, the Talmud, says that a person "is known by his pocket, his cup and his rage."[5] Too many of us are known for our indifference. One scholar of religion notes that we have "a smorgasbord religiosity whose primary aim seems to be to make us feel good about God but god forbid that this should place any demands on us."[6] A visitor to the United States commented, "I notice your churches have cushions"—suggesting our wealth—and then he added, "I notice your preaching has cushions too"—meaning that we tread lightly on expectations of how we apply our professions of religious belief toward the causes of justice and helping the poor.

What is needed, because it is generally lacking, is a real sense of commitment, a willingness to stand up, to do the extra "little things" that committed people do, whether they win each battle or not. Bread for the World, a Christian-oriented policy group that works on hunger problems, says that its 1995 campaign "to protect crucial development aid to Africa mobilized approximately 70,000 letters and reduced by $100 million the cuts that took place."[7] Each letter probably saved a life. The annual *Status Report on Hunger and Homelessness* issued by U.S. mayors at the end of 2001 says that both hunger and homelessness in this nation are rising. Do we just sit back and say, "too bad"? Or do we do something about that? Isolated individuals are not likely to do anything. They need guidance; they need to sense they are part of a team effort that is getting something done. That's where solid leadership by the faith community can play a vital role. Religion historian Martin Marty notes, "Unless religious impulses find a home in more than the individual heart . . . they will have few long-lasting public consequences."[8] The good news is that people who are actively connected with an organized religion are much more likely to volunteer for causes, give blood to the Red Cross, help Habitat for Humanity, and do other noble things. However, someone must ask them!

If people are requested to do things, aren't they more likely to avoid the organization that made the request, whether it is religious or secular? Sometimes that will happen, but more typically, as they become active and see constructive things happen, they increase their activity and enthusiasm. One non-Mormon observed of the Church of Jesus Christ of Latter-day Saints, one of the few religious bodies showing substantial membership gains in the United States: "The high requirement of giving of time and talent appears to work in a positive way. . . . Many churches don't require much. You go when you want and you give what you want. That doesn't inspire loyalty—that's a casual club."[9]

But few new people are choosing to join these clubs. A declining percentage of young people show an interest in organized religion, and my nonscientific reading from talking with many of them suggests two reasons: First, the claim by some religious bodies to have a monopoly on truth turns them off, and second, young people don't see religion, as they observe its practices, as relevant to their lives or their world. Some fundamentalist groups in all faiths are growing, and I sense that, in part, it is because they demand some sacrifice by their adherents, but the rigidity of their messages does not appeal to most young people. One author notes: "Religion may have a salutary effect on civil society by encouraging its members to worship, to spend time with their families, and to learn the moral lessons embedded in religious traditions. But religion is likely to have a diminished impact on society if that is the only role it plays."[10] It is also less likely to appeal to bright young people. William Bennett, former vice president of Boston University, says of the school, "'This is a Methodist institution, but the student body is one-third Catholic, one-third Jewish and one-third Protestant, two-thirds of whom don't believe in anything."[11] Part of that is natural youthful skepticism, but my contact with students suggests that part of it is they see nothing vital, nothing earth-moving, nothing courageously constructive in the religious communities that they observe. For the most part, they are right.

People occasionally comment that our federal government should not give foreign aid for economic development because that responsibility should be left to the religious and charitable organizations. Dare we leave something so crucial entirely in the hands of faith groups? Lutheran World Relief is the principal charitable arm for eight million Lutherans. Divide the membership into the amount Lutheran World Relief receives from them annually, and it amounts to slightly more than one-half of one cent per person per day. That level of contribution does good things, but it is hardly a sacrifice by mostly middle-income Lutherans. What is true of Lutherans is true of most major religious bodies, with the exception of the Friends (Quakers), the Mennonites, the Brethren, and the Seventh Day Adventists. These sums help to aid an underdeveloped or underfed country but by themselves are woefully inadequate.

But good things can happen. The small congregation to which I belong in Carbondale, Illinois, has a socially sensitive pastor, Robert Gray. A few years ago, when the Honduran floods came, he headed efforts to get help. The church body to which the congregation belongs (Missouri Synod Lutheran) represents approximately one-third of all Lutherans in the United States. The church periodical later reported that this one-third of Lutherandom contributed $135,000 to Honduran flood relief. Thanks to Pastor Gray, our congregation—usually about one hundred fifty attend each Sunday—with the help of others in the community collected $130,000 in cash, clothing, blankets, and drugs for the flood victims—almost as much as one-third of all U.S. Lutherans, with 2.7 million members.

Positive things are happening as a result of the leadership of local religious groups—food kitchens, housing for the desperate, and nursing home care are just a few examples—and nationally, through organizations like Bread for the World, Catholic Relief Services, United Jewish Federations, World Vision, Network (run by Catholic nuns), and an almost endless list that is both heartening and discouraging: heartening because of the good that is being done, discouraging when compared to the potential. For every congregation that is doing something significant, there are more than thirty (my conservative guess) that are largely coasting, paying lip service to living their faith but not much more, and their "leaders" are doing little to awaken them. One of my friends calls it "counterfeit compassion," meaning that it is composed of dormant good will but doesn't get any results as real compassion would.

Still, we must give credit to those who are trying, and it would be easy to compile a long list of heartwarming examples of what religious groups have done and are doing. In Philadelphia, for example, churches, synagogues, and secular groups have joined —with the help of the Pew Charitable Trusts—to provide reading assistance programs for inner-city youth. While the numbers are small compared to the need, children who have taken part for six months or more have lifted their grade reading level by 1.9 years.

In lower Manhattan in New York City, the Episcopal Church of the Apostles, with less than two hundred members, last year provided 285,000 meals for indigent people, and perhaps as significant as the meals, they report that "the entire congregation is involved in it."[12] Founded in 1841, the church dwindled to twenty-five or thirty attending services each Sunday. The bishop made clear that the church might close. In the meantime, hungry people were knocking on the door of the church office asking for food. The pastor decided to try to raise $50,000 to feed people. Now they feed almost a thousand people a day, the largest single feeding program in New York City. They raise $2 million a year for food assistance, largely through the mail. About one hundred fifty members of the church are involved, plus fifty volunteers and a staff of twenty-eight. In 1990, they suffered a bad fire, and because of the unusual work of the church, it made the front page of the *New York Times* and local television and radio outlets. The day after the fire, they fed 943 people by candlelight. That made the news again, and money started pouring in. "The church rose from the ashes," Father William Greenlaw, its pastor, reports. "The feeding program has given life back to our parish." They now have a $7 million church and physical facility. So often, assistance is through a check, a good but antiseptic method of helping that avoids contact with the grime and struggle that poor people face. When the poor and not-poor meet face-to-face, another meeting also takes place: public policy and the needs of people.

The same day I talked to Father Greenlaw on the phone, I received a mail appeal from Rev. Julio Loza of St. Matthew Lutheran Church on the West Side of Chicago. One staff person, Maria Leal, and some volunteers prepare and serve the meals at St. Matthew's. Maria also counsels the women who come. The appeal notes that it is "the only faith-based community outreach program in the Northern Illinois District" of the Missouri Synod of the Lutheran Church.[13] That district has 245 affiliated Lutheran congregations.

Those two churches with vastly differing situations are helping desperate people. As examples, they are encouraging for what they do but discouraging when we realize how many others are doing nothing or next to nothing.

Discouraging also is the widening gap between the more fortunate and the less fortunate within the United States and the growing differential between the standard of living of Americans and the rest of the world. In 1999, *Business Week* noted: "What's happening is that a new class of left-behind workers is being created [in the United States], encompassing a large portion of the workforce. They have jobs, sometimes with high salaries, but while their New Economy counterparts' earnings soar, the left-behinds are struggling to post small real gains in income. That's why, despite the overall prosperity, many households keep taking on more debt."[14] But the problem is more than one within our borders.

Robert Fogel of the University of Chicago says, "Every populist movement in the United States that has been of enough scope to get into the history books has had a religious underpinning."[15] Can there be a popular "uprising" that demands that our faith groups and government be more responsive to the needs of the poor in our nation and in other nations? Or will the powerful tool of applied religion largely gather dust in a world that cries for greater response from the comfortable and largely aloof United States?

A few years ago, I read an article—and I regret I do not recall who wrote it or where it appeared—in which the author analyzed inner-city churches and concluded that those churches that have survival as their main goal generally don't survive, while those that have service as their goal survive. A book titled *Excellent Protestant Congregations* notes that many churches have choirs, biking clubs, bowling teams, and other social activities but also have concrete avenues of service for the congregants. The author notes: "All excellent churches see their work as not only serving their constituency but also transforming the world around them. These churches are willing to go into the world and to affect the civic and social structure. They do it out of the biblical mandate and with biblical standards, not merely to be power brokers."[16] Yet so many are indifferent.

When Hitler came to power in Germany, that nation's population, almost half Lutheran and half Catholic, accepted him, in part, because most of their religious leaders said they wanted to "stay out of politics," and that was all tyranny needed. The churches took that stance despite Hitler's words in *Mein Kampf*: "I believe that I am acting in accordance with the will of the Almighty Creator: By defending myself against the Jews, I am fighting for the Lord."[17] But Lutherans and Catholics were not alone in their indifference. The Baptist World Alliance held its congress in Berlin in 1934, and its official report notes, "Chancellor Adolf Hitler gives . . . the prestige of his personal example since he neither uses intoxicants nor smokes."[18] The president of the Southern Baptist Theological Seminary in Louisville,

Kentucky, criticized "too hasty judgment of a leader who has stopped German women from smoking cigarettes and wearing red lipstick in public."[19] A delegate to the conference, a Baptist minister from Boston, wrote: "It was a great relief to be in a country where salacious literature cannot be sold. . . . The new Germany has burned great masses of corrupting books and magazines along with its bonfires of Jewish and communistic libraries."[20] We look back smugly and believe we would have done better, shown more courage. But when UNICEF reports that around the world, 9,500 children a day die because of poor quality water—easily preventable deaths—we do not stir ourselves, or only barely do. Again, there are small efforts, like the Marion Medical Mission from southern Illinois, that has volunteers who go to Malawi in southern Africa to help people there construct water wells that are safer. Having 9,500 children a day die because of unsafe water should startle us. That's 630 times as many as were gunned down at Columbine High School in Colorado, more than three times as many as died in the senseless tragedy of September 11. But we hardly notice. Religious leaders, whose professed faith allegiance should cause them to admonish the indifferent, as the Old Testament prophet Amos once did, are generally silent. A Roman Catholic writer notes, "In a holy life, the applecart is always upset."[21]

We somehow think we are "being religious" when we add the words "under God" to the Pledge of Allegiance or get into a dispute about trying to post the Ten Commandments at a local school, but the real test of faith is not what we mouth but what we do. An active local lay religious leader, Roland Keim, told me that religion is "more caught than taught."

I am old enough to have participated in the civil rights movement, and in that endeavor we had admonitions from most of the mainline Christian and Jewish branches urging action against the cruelties and crudities of legal segregation as practiced openly in the South and less openly in the North. "This is a moral issue," they properly asserted. But most individual congregations and local church leaders remained silent, while a sizable minority—and a majority in the South—defended the practice of segregation. Martin Luther King, a Baptist minister, led a bloodless revolution that changed the face of our nation for the better. But I remember going to Montgomery at his invitation to speak at the second anniversary of the bus boycott and finding only two white ministers in the Montgomery area who were willing to identify publicly with Dr. King and his cause. His story reveals both the power that religion can have and the weakness of too many in leadership positions who pander to their constituents. Church leaders intoned, "There is no scriptural admonition against segregation," and technically, that is correct. No precise language in Christian and Jewish scriptures forbids segregation, but many religious leaders and journals agreed that segregation violated the spirit of basic faith creeds. The opposition of a substantial number to any proclamation on the issue stirred debate and caused the religious proponents of change to become more zealous in their advocacy. Almost the same thing happened before the Civil War on the issue of slavery, when some asserted that there is no scriptural admonition "Thou shalt not have slaves." But the Wesleys in England and their many counterparts in the United States, particularly among the Friends (Quakers), took strong stands that slavery violated the precepts of Christian and Jewish faiths, the two religious groups with significant numbers in the United States then. The eagerness by both sides to convince the other reduced the level of indifference.

On the issue of poverty, the basic documents of Christians, Jews, Muslims, Hindus, Buddhists, and other groups all strongly advocate helping the poor. There is no opposition. But there is massive indifference, and the lack of outright hostility to helping the poor reduces attention to the issue, both within the religious communities and with the public at large. Maybe we need a few people to shout at us, "Don't help the poor!" Perhaps that would awaken us from our slumber. I wish once a year all of us could walk through the lobby of the United Nations Building to read the words of Mahatma Gandhi: "Recall the face of the poorest and weakest man you have seen and ask yourself if the step you contemplate is going to be of any use to him."

People of all faiths might ask themselves, Why is the Salvation Army so highly regarded, receiving support from many who differ with their theology? We know the answer. At the Public Policy Institute I head at Southern Illinois University, we had a symposium to look at the faith community and the challenge of domestic poverty. Participants ranged from Imam Wallace Mohammed, a Muslim leader, to Rabbi Jacob Rubenstein, then head of the Orthodox Rabbinical Council of America, to Dr. John Buehrens, then head of the Unitarian Universalist Church Association, to Dr. Pat Robertson, the prominent television evangelist. People started the discussions with widely divergent views on *how* to deal with the issue, but gradually they came together and issued a strong statement. There has been some follow-through, the Seventh Day Adventists doing a better job on this than any other group, though scattered and less consistent responses have occurred from others. Again, perhaps the response would have been much more vigorous if there were theologians and philosophers who disagreed with the idea that we should reach out with a helping hand of opportunity to the most miserable in our society and beyond our borders. Saying that we should help the poor is about as controversial as saying that two and two are four. No serious person questions either assumption. But *how* we help and *how much* we help are questions too infrequently addressed, and on those questions there are legitimate points of disagreement. Author Barbara Ehrenreich says, "Ours is a society that routinely generates destitution—and then, perversely, relieves its conscience by vilifying the destitute."[22]

In the absence of concrete leadership from those who should bestir our collective conscience, Congress and presidential administrations have let our response to the world's hopeless gradually descend to its present low status. I saw no religious leader or journalist comment on the inaccuracy of President George W. Bush's statement in China early in 2002 that the United States provides more aid to the world's poor than any other nation. I wish that statement were accurate. In absolute dollars, it is false —with France and Japan, nations with less than half our population, contributing more in absolute dollars; and as I pointed out in an earlier chapter, the United States trails in last place among the twenty-two wealthiest nations in terms of the percentage of our national income or tax dollar that goes to help the poor beyond our borders. Norway, Denmark, and the Netherlands each contribute more than seven times what we do as a percentage of income.

At a meeting of the World Economic Forum gathered in New York City four months after the events of September 11, Secretary of State Colin Powell told those assembled that to deal effectively with terrorism we have to recognize that it breeds easily among those who are impoverished and hopeless. He is right, of course. A few weeks later, the president's budget went to Congress, requesting $48 *billion* more in defense and $800 *million* more for aid to the world's poor—only one-sixtieth as much of an increase for developmental assistance as for defense. We were already—before the $48 billion increase—spending more on arms than the next eight nations combined. I support a strong defense. But is this rational spending? The *New York Times* reports that if the president's requested defense increase is approved, we will spend more on arms in FY 2004 than all the other nations in the world combined, not counting the Iraq war expenditures.[23] Based on figures from the Center for Defense Information, the *Times* statement is a slight exaggeration. Their figures show we will spend more than the next top twenty-six nations combined on defense.

However, we lag behind all the other wealthy nations in helping the world's poor. If the president's request is accepted for the $800 million increase for the impoverished—and Congress is likely to reduce it—foreign economic aid still will total less than one-half of 1 percent of our budget. Compounding this inadequacy, at a meeting in New York of the western European nations, Japan, Canada, the United States, and UN officials, the suggestion was made that over the next few years donor countries double their assistance to the poor, a total increase for all nations of $50 billion, or slightly more than the *one year increase* in the U.S. defense budget. The other nations favored the idea. The United States vetoed it. That barely made the news; I read about it in only one newspaper—but it received much greater attention abroad. That veto would not have happened if faith leaders in our nation had pushed vigorously for help. There was enough adverse reaction *from other nations* to the veto of more aid by the United States that the president made a speech at a multinational gathering in Monterey, Mexico, calling for more developmental assistance by the wealthier nations. He suggested a $5 billion increase by the United States over the next three years, a welcome gesture. But nothing I have read or heard has suggested that U.S. religious leaders played a prominent role in bringing about the Monterey address. A few weeks later, an e-mail went to all of the clergy of the Lutheran Church's Missouri Synod. The message:

> On rare occasions urgent matters are brought to the attention of ordained and commissioned ministers . . . through a "Call-to-Action." In this "Call-to-Action" I encourage you to contact your U.S. Senators in support of a new congressional bill that is intended to protect the housing allowance available to both ordained and commissioned ministers of the Gospel. . . . The Court of Appeals may . . . find the housing allowance unconstitutional. . . . Legislation has been

passed in the House of Representatives (H.R. 4156) in an attempt to protect the housing allowance.[24]

Has a similar urgent appeal gone to these same members of the clergy with a "Call-to-Action" to pass or improve the feeble U.S. response to world poverty? Not that anyone can recall.

The organization Bread for the World estimates that ending hunger in the United States, and for the United States to do its share to cut hunger in half abroad in the next fifteen years, would cost approximately eleven cents per day for each U.S. citizen. Kenneth Hackett, executive director of Catholic Relief Services, says, "Feeding the world is not a big *money* thing. It's a big *will* thing."[25] A University of Maryland survey of national attitudes noted that "83 percent said they believed the United States should join an international program to cut world hunger in half by 2015, and 75 percent would be willing to pay an extra $50 in taxes per year to achieve it."[26] The response to this and all polls is partially tilted by how questions are asked. But the survey makes clear that if presidential and legislative leadership had the courage to appeal to the noble in us, we would respond.

Other nations look upon the United States as a Christian nation, even though we have religious diversity, just as we look upon Jordan, for example, as a Muslim nation, even though it tolerates religious diversity. While the insensitivity to the rest of the world reflects on all Americans, it also reflects on how, in the field of religion, we practice what we profess. Just as callous behavior on our part reflects unfavorably on democracy in the eyes of many outside our borders, so slumbering indifference to poverty by religious believers is viewed by many as a major flaw in whatever beliefs we profess to embrace.

Here is the heading on a news story: "Fire Kills 3 Kids, 4 Adults in Poverty-Stricken Family."[27] The article makes clear that poverty within the United States killed them. The Associated

Press carried another small story that claimed, "Poor women are less likely to be diagnosed and treated for breast cancer, and more likely to die from it, according to a study that searched for reasons why fewer black women survive the disease than whites."[28] We must learn to read items like these as a challenge to our political beliefs and our creedal professions. Centuries before Jesus or Muhammad, the prophet Amos wrote that because people denied justice to the oppressed, the Lord despised their religious assemblies, their songs, and their sacrifices.[29]

Why don't adherents of various faiths do more to meet the needs of the disadvantaged and to create bridges of tolerance and understanding? Part of the reason is simply human frailty. None of us lives up to the ideals we embrace. But it is more than that. Part of it is that we are comfortable with the status quo. That is true of the majority of "leaders" in any field. But it is also more than that. *We are mesmerized by numbers.*

To be a pastor or rabbi or imam for a congregation with a thousand members provides greater status (and usually a better salary) than being the spiritual leader for one hundred fifty members. Sometimes those numbers are important, but they should not be a substitute for quality of service. Leaders should not pander to the whims of people to build up numbers if that comfort is a substitute for applying faith to life. A Methodist minister, John Annable, writes, "It is encouraging to hear our bishops now tell clergy to stop counting members and start making disciples."[30] When pandering becomes the means to keep the numbers high, something is dramatically wrong. In her book *Broken Tablets,* Rabbi Rachel Mikva speaks about the need "to unite a [religious] community around common obligations rather than common interests."[31] The temptation to entertain instead of providing substance is not only a temptation for the media. Examples of common interests in a congregation might be dart ball leagues, bowling or softball activities, quilting gatherings, and much more—all good interests, but too often they substitute for our responsibility to meet the common obligations. Common interests may bring in more numbers. Common obligations may, in rare circumstances, even diminish numbers, though that theory is not tested often. Hartford Seminary in Connecticut surveyed fourteen thousand congregations, and most of the conclusions drawn from it are not startling, but one is of more than modest importance: "Congregations that enact their faith, without explicit expectations for members, experience less vitality and more conflict."[32]

Two years ago, I spoke to a regional convention in Minnesota of the Evangelical Lutheran Church of America, the larger of the two major Lutheran bodies. During the presentation, I asked that seven congregations volunteer to make an annual report, not only on baptisms, confirmations, weddings, funerals, and church membership and not only on how much money is in the bank and whether the roof leaks; but that they also remember the story that Jesus told in which he asked questions about responding to the needs of the impoverished (Matthew 25: 31–45). I asked the seven congregations to specifically identify what they were doing for the poor, the thirsty, the hungry, the outcast, the sick, and those in prison.

One congregation has written to me saying that taking this path got them involved in a healthy self-examination. At the convention, one pastor commented to me that the churches that volunteered were the congregations that already had shown sensitivity, and that the ones who needed it the most did not volunteer. Whether that is true or not, I do not know.

What I do know is that the leaders of every faith call for action, whether Jesus, or the prophets Isaiah or Amos, or Muhammad, in these words from the Qur'an: "It is not righteous that you turn your faces to the East or West, but righteous is he who believes in Allah . . . and gives his wealth . . . to orphans and the needy and the wayfarer and to those who ask, and sets slaves free."[33]

It is easy for religious leaders of any persuasion to avoid

disturbing things. The culture in which we live can smother the possibility of asking ourselves penetrating questions. The religious routine—or perhaps more accurately, the irreligious routine—lets the pastor or priest or rabbi or imam pander to the members of his or her flock who live in comfort, ignoring the needs of those whom their faith suggests we should aid.

Part of our problem is that we isolate ourselves and have trouble meeting and working with people of other faiths. Major religions are a combination of reality and tradition, and history shapes and twists both. That twisting gets exaggerated as extreme statements are picked up by the media. At a national gathering in Dallas, a former president of the Southern Baptist Convention, Rev. Jerry Vines, made a speech in which he called the prophet of Islam, Muhammad, a "demon-infested pedophile."[34] I am sure he felt that his remarks advanced the cause of Christianity, just as Muslim extremists do when they say outlandish things that distort the public image of Islam or other faiths. History too often focuses on attacks suffered by "our" religion and builds hatred and fear. Israel's thoughtful and eloquent Abba Eban wrote, "We live intimately with the past, but the past is the enemy of the future."[35] That is true, not only in the Middle East. We must learn from history but should not be captured by it. Imam Abdul Haqq writes, "If we can put aside differences to make a great university, a great car or a great business, surely we can do the same to . . . develop the best individuals and society while maintaining our excellent individual religious traditions."[36]

This small story is heartening:

> Trinity Lutheran Church, Lynwood, Wash., will share a "Good Neighbor Award" with St. Thomas More Roman Catholic parish and The Assembly Dar Alarqam mosque. The award, presented by the nonprofit group Search for Common Ground, recognizes the three congregations'

> effort to encourage worship at the mosque after it was vandalized following the Sept. 11, 2001, attacks. More than 100 Lynwood-area Christians stood guard outside the mosque and welcomed worshipers the Friday after the attacks.[37]

There are too few examples like that, in part because religion leaders often live in isolation from one another, and the small gestures needed after September 11 seemed awkward to them. That is the reason we need to listen—really listen—to others. American author and philosopher Elbert Hubbard early in the last century said, "To know but one religion is not to know that one."[38] In the Israeli town of Gilboa, forty-eight Arab and Jewish seventh to ninth grade students took part in a quiz contest in which Arabs were questioned about the Torah (Jewish scriptures) and Jews were questioned about the Qur'an. From what might have been a boring lecture for many young people, it turned into an exciting learning experience, not just for the forty-eight contestants but for the other young people listening to the quiz.[39]

In 1991, someone brutally murdered six Buddhist monks and three lay Buddhists in Arizona. It caused the Arizona Ecumenical Council to issue these "10 Commandments of Religious Pluralism":

> 1. Make a conscious effort to *identify all* ethnic and religious minority groups in your community.
>
> 2. Research in advance their culture, history, art, religion. Demonstrating some specific knowledge suggests honest interest. Ignorance is insulting.
>
> 3. Be intentional about contacting them. Do not be put off by initial expressions of discomfort or distrust. Repeat the contacts as opportunities arise.
>
> 4. Respect their basic humanity. Do not see them as foreigners or competitors for jobs. "Have we not all one father? Has not one God created us?" (Malachi 2:20)

5. Respect their independence but not to the point of indifference. Fear of interfering may be seen as lack of interest and sincerity.

6. Respect individuality. Not all members of the same nationality are exactly alike.

7. Be specific. Avoid generalizations, stereotypes, assumptions.

8. Do not mistake apologies about difficulty with the English language, their refugee status or poverty as expressions of cultural inferiority. They have pride, too.

9. Understand their perception of nationality and religion as synonymous. Our concept of the separation of church and state is unusual and may be foreign to them. Our "sin" of denominational division may be even more difficult for them to understand.

10. Analyze honestly many of our own customs and practices. It will make you much more tolerant of theirs.[40]

We shouldn't need murder to encourage our trying to understand those who differ from us. These suggestions are good.

In reaching out to understand the beliefs of others, there is often fear that exposure to "other ideas" might taint the faith of "our people." Because we rarely listen to those of differing faith communities, we accept the belief that "we are right, and they are wrong," and that historically has too often disintegrated into "we're good, they're bad." Bitterness and violence often follow.

It is strange that in the world of politics we rarely articulate the theological argument about sin and error being part of the deliberative process, but as you enter into a dispute on the floor of the U.S. Senate or in a presidential debate, there usually is a civility that is sometimes lacking in religious encounters. What is true in debates and discussions is not true of political advertisements. For whatever reason, religious ads are civil, but religious debates are often uncivil. In politics, the ads are frequently uncivil, the debate civil. Most of us enter a political debate aware that there is at least a remote possibility that "my" interpretation of reality may be wrong. It usually tempers what is said. In the world of religion, those who have plumbed the depths of understanding about sin and error as part of humanity too often do not apply that possibility to their own interpretation of ultimate realities. And so the disputant in a religious debate—particularly within a denomination—faces greater rigidities, for each side claims that he or she has an insight into what God wants. So you may be arguing, in a sense, with God rather than another equally flawed mortal. However, most interfaith dialogues "are very respectful," notes Rabbi David Saperstein of Washington, D.C., a participant in many of them.[41] However, because religious insights are so emotionally defended, often genuine conversation about beliefs never takes place, even though there may be pleasant but superficial encounters.

Religion can make more of a difference for those who need help, and faith groups working together to meet those needs end up with an improved relationship and inevitably an increased interest in public policy. Aloofness from the political scene once advocated by religious leaders has gradually diminished. Fundamentalist Christians who once paid little attention to policy making have shifted to form organizations such as the Moral Majority and the Christian Coalition, both of them currently diminishing in influence but with a residue of increased belief on the part of their followers that political involvement is a positive good. I differ with both groups on many policies; I hope they develop a greater respect for diversity and for the motives of those who oppose them. However, the shift in attitude toward greater civic participation is healthy.

In western Europe, there has not been this same aloofness, the Holocaust having shaken any belief that quiescence is somehow desirable. Political parties even carry names such as Christian Democrats, though there are no direct ties in most cases to any church or theological positions.

There is frequently a public bow to religion by our national leaders, usually—as I sense—for political purposes. Religion can be a unifying factor for the nation, but too often on these public occasions it is exploited. However, who can question the sincerity of George Washington's farewell address, in which he speaks of the importance of religion, or the sensitive comments of Abraham Lincoln in his second inaugural address? Lincoln, perhaps the most theologically profound of our presidents, attended church services regularly but was the only president not to have a religious affiliation.

Religious affiliation generally has not dictated the actions of public officials. Roman Catholic judges grant divorces, for example. I had a debate at the University of Chicago with Supreme Court Justice Antonin Scalia, a Roman Catholic, on the issue of capital punishment in which I, a Lutheran, sided with the position of the Catholic Church, and he did not. Southern Baptists were regularly unhappy with Presidents Jimmy Carter and Bill Clinton. In the case of Jimmy Carter, the unhappiness went both ways, and he later disassociated himself from the Southern Baptist Convention because of the stand it took in opposition to allowing women in the clergy. Episcopal leadership opposed the Gulf War when our commander-in-chief, the senior President George Bush, belonged to that church. These illustrations do not mean that religious leadership is powerless. It can affect, but rarely totally determines, policy making.

In addition to talking to and working with political leaders, what effective, constructive things can religious leaders do? The preacher, whatever his or her formal title, should make clear to the congregants that faith must be applied to life, that there are obligations that are not fulfilled by attending regular worship services or fasting or praying five times a day. For most groups, the only sacrifice that the leader asks the flock to make is to contribute more to the local budget. That is part of the obligation but only part of it. There is no shortage of admonitions to reach out to the dispossessed and the miserable from the recognized holy writings of every religion.

Ordinarily, the weekly exhortation should stir but not be too specific. For example, no one should ignore the forty-three million Americans who have no health insurance, but people can have honest differences on how to reach them. So the leader ordinarily should not present himself or herself as an expert with the remedy, though different faith traditions have great variations in tolerating candid specifics from their leaders. What is not tolerable is for the problem to be ignored. A sermon that includes references to this issue needs follow-through. The difficulty in most faith groups is that we do not even get to phase one, having a sermon reference on the subject. Leaders are afraid it might offend someone. It might, but usually it will not, if handled properly.

Then the congregation's spiritual leader should discuss with key members of the group how they can follow through. On the issue of world hunger, for example, Christians have an organization that speaks to government called Bread for the World, based in Washington. There are numerous religiously affiliated relief agencies and other organizations that could suggest an action agenda.

Within each congregation, there is often a men's club or a women's organization or a breakfast club or a social action group. Get that entity together to brainstorm how they and others in the congregation can effectively influence policy. You may run into some who say, "Separation of church and state. The church should not be politically involved." But remember, that's what many said when Hitler rose to power in Germany. People who have faith values should communicate their concerns to political leaders, not with a self-righteous we-have-all-the-answers attitude but as concerned citizens. Having a group discussion with key members will be healthy. Good ideas will emerge from such a session. That group discussion could lead to doing any of the following things among its starters:

- Get members to volunteer for a homeless shelter, or for an area mental health cause, to visit an inner-city neighborhood and give a few Saturdays or other time to work with drug addicts or to mentor children who need help in school, or to help Habitat for Humanity. There are literally hundreds of good causes yearning for assistance. Independent Sector, a coalition of more than eight hundred voluntary groups, found that "those households with one or more volunteers gave an average of $1,193 [to charitable causes] while households that gave money but had no volunteers gave an average of $425."[42] We have been told that where our treasure is, there will our heart be, but the reverse is also true. If we see and learn about a compelling need, our treasure—at least a little of it—will follow.
- Sponsor a debate/discussion between the candidates running for the U.S. House on the question of foreign aid and the elimination of domestic poverty. Have at least two or three of your members well prepared to ask penetrating questions. Make sure you work hard at getting a crowd. The idea that there will automatically be a good turnout for the appearance of people who are prominent in the news is usually not accurate. Serving food usually helps increase the crowd and improve the atmosphere. Your speakers will be more impressed if you have a room or hall or religious edifice packed with people. It is important when holding a candidate forum that all candidates be invited, and it should be structured in such a way that does not suggest support or opposition to any candidate by the sponsoring organization. In a nonelection year, invite an officeholder to visit with your group on a designated topic.

• Sponsor a debate/discussion between candidates for your state legislature on mental health, prison reform, or other subjects.

• After each of these meetings, arrange for letters—from individuals, not from the organization—to be sent to the candidates and to other officeholders. Make sure you follow through on this. Most people say they will write a letter and then do not. I recently asked someone in a key position to get twenty letters to her state senator. She said she would. I later checked with the state senator. He had received two letters.

You could even skip the debate and simply concentrate on getting letters to candidates. The key is to act. Concentrate on two or three issues at the most. If you write on twelve topics, you dissipate the effect. Keep the letter short, one page if possible, two at the most. Your lawmakers and their staffs are busy and are not likely to do more than glance at a long letter. Officeholders do not expect you to know all the details on issues, but they are interested in knowing your concerns. If you don't contact them, those who contribute generously to the candidates probably will set the agenda.

You could also write a short but carefully worded letter to the editor of your local newspaper. Every survey shows that letters to the editor are read more than editorials. It is a way to influence both the public and officeholders.

Frequently, the religious leader of the local congregation may feel uncomfortable taking on these nontraditional functions. A lay member could volunteer to assist or lead, easing into a more responsible role for the group.

Issues often also offer an opportunity to get different faith groups to work together. Almost inevitably, working together results in more understanding than other formal or even informal exchanges. We come to understand that we have differences, but we share so much. We need to learn to respect and tolerate our differences and also learn how much we have in common. Bridges must be built, and they can be started at the congregation level.

In 1978, shortly after the war in Vietnam ended, President Jimmy Carter appointed me one of the delegates to a United Nations session. While there, I tried to meet people I could not meet on the Washington scene, so I invited the Vietnamese delegation to lunch. At that point, relations between our two nations were frigid. During the lunch, it became clear that they wanted to improve their status with the United States, and I got permission for them to come to Washington, D.C. (Representatives of nations we view as hostile are not permitted to go more than twenty-five miles outside the United Nations.) A few members of Congress from both parties and representatives of the State Department met with the Vietnamese at my Washington home. My then-seventeen-year-old daughter Sheila listened to our conversation from the stairway near our living room, taking in the scene with fascination. Afterwards, she remarked, "It's hard to believe we were fighting them."

Once we see our common humanity, it is hard to look at people as enemies, whether they are from another nation, another race, or another religion. If violence in the world is to diminish, we must understand that basic lesson. Exchanges in the field of religion will not occur unless someone plans, someone leads. This may take a little courage. It demands more than silence. There is an unspoken and inaccurate belief on the part of many that silence in some vague way can lead to understanding, or at least tolerance. That is inaccurate. During my early years in the state legislature, the teacher placement office of the University of Illinois found in a survey that only one-fourth of the school administrators in our state were willing to employ a Jew and an even smaller percentage, an African American. Attitudes—and the law—have changed since then, fortunately. Attitude change followed the change in the law, but silence did not change the law.

Even a small thing can become significant. Sometimes when I speak to an audience, I say, "Too many white families here have never had an African American family to their home for dinner. Too many African American families have never had a white family to their home for dinner." I often give other examples, including some across faith barriers. When I mention these things, the audience becomes totally silent—and I know that I have touched a raw nerve. Doing this simple act requires approval of no organization or denomination, and it can enlarge horizons and build greater understanding.

To help achieve this understanding, we must learn more about the cultures that have helped shape the people with whom we are trying to communicate. For instance, the militancy and even the cruelty of Muslim extremists is frequently mentioned in these post–September 11 days. One reason it does exist is that in many Muslim nations the self-restraint that comes with freedom of speech and other freedoms is often not present. Self-restraint does not guarantee responsible conduct, but it makes it more probable. A fascinating and insightful document, *The Arab Human Development Report 2002*, sponsored by the Arab Fund for Economic and Social Development of the United Nations, is startling in its frankness about how the lack of freedom in many Arab nations has retarded their economic and intellectual growth.[43] Written by a distinguished group of Arab scholars, its candor is refreshing and in the long run will be helpful. All cultures and religions need this type of no-holds-barred self-examination. In Freedom House's annual survey of liberty, seven of the ten countries listed as the most repressive governments are Muslim nations. This statistic seems to reinforce those who say that Muslims cannot handle freedom. But I remember when virtually all Latin American nations had dictatorships, and a few of the State Department elites ridiculed President Jimmy Carter's appeal for human rights. "Latin Americans by temperament and culture aren't attuned for free systems," they intoned. Today, there is only one complete dictatorship left in Latin America. Now the same semi-informed elites are giving us the same line about Arab or Muslim nations. A full-blown and stable democracy will not appear anywhere overnight, but the craving for freedom and a better life is universal, whether the nation is Christian, Muslim, Jewish, Hindu, Buddhist, animist, or nonreligious. Having a free system—and sometimes it has to emerge step by step—encourages stability, and when that is evident, it brings investment that adds to productivity and to a higher standard of living. Nations with temporarily high standards of living because of oil must look to the future. Even that great oil income is starting to turn sour. Saudi Arabia has an 18 percent unemployment rate and a much higher rate for those under forty, the bulk of their population. That is potentially explosive. Muslim nations constitute 20 percent of the world's population but only 4 percent of the world's trade. More democratic governments will change that.

Stable democracies also are peaceful neighbors. As Harvard scholar Amarty Sen points out, "No famine has ever taken place in the history of the world in a functioning democracy—be it economically rich or relatively poor."[44] In free countries, ugly and unfounded rumors can be punctured with truth. Freedom does not by itself guarantee restraint. Lynchings took place in this nation, usually not for religious reasons, but freedom did not stop this cruelty for decades. Hindu and Muslim extremists have slaughtered untold numbers in freedom-loving India. But extremist acts are less likely when people can talk freely about their concerns, when prejudices and false reports have a chance to be reduced by openly airing ideas, good and bad.

However, Christians who speak from a "holier-than-thou" perspective about Muslim actions can read the history of Christian nations before the emergence of freedom—and even afterwards—and note embarrassing cruelties. The 1994 genocide in Rwanda in Central Africa in which eight hundred thousand to one million people were slaughtered took place in a nation that is nominally 90 percent Christian. The forced baptism of Jews in eighth-century Spain, on penalty of execution, is but one of a myriad of examples that can be cited of people from virtually every religious background. Look at the last decade: Hindu mobs in India attacked and killed Muslims. Muslims in northern Nigeria killed and pillaged Christian minorities. In what once was a larger Yugoslavia, Orthodox Christians of the Eastern Rites and Roman Catholic Christians frequently faced each other over the barrel of a gun and destroyed each other's churches. In the Sudan, a woman is sentenced to death by stoning for committing adultery, based on Muslim law. In the largely Christian United States, we execute more people than all but two other nations, and since the Supreme Court reinstated the death penalty in 1976, thirty-five mentally retarded people with an IQ below seventy have been put to death after being found guilty of murder. The stories, unfortunately, are almost endless.

The words of some icons of religion that are less than violent (but that often lead to violence) are discouraging. Some of Martin Luther's comments about Jews were shameful, and reading the transcript of the widely respected Billy Graham's conversation with President Richard Nixon about Jews, we squirm with embarrassment for Dr. Graham, who had the good sense to apologize.

As I write this book, Muslim fanaticism concerns us more than any other form of extremism, but all major religions have had their embarrassing and shocking violent eruptions of fanaticism. After the bloody Crusades of the eleventh and twelfth centuries, launched by Christians, "small" slights were noted in Arabic textbooks, such as the use of one of the holiest Muslim sites, the al-Aqsa mosque, as a stable for the horses of the Crusaders. It made President George W. Bush's use of the word "crusade" in a speech describing our response to the September 11 attack particularly unfortunate, since he intended no ill will toward followers of

Islam. Those of almost every faith who practice fanaticism find passages in their holy writings to justify violence, passages taken out of context. It may be true, as Graham Fuller, an expert on Islam, suggests, that while some Islamic movements are moving toward greater moderation, "much of the Islamic community is heading in the other direction, growing more austere and less tolerant."[45]

Dr. Mazhar Butt, a Muslim leader who travels widely, told me he disagrees with that assessment. He believes that the views of extremists are being given great attention but that most Muslims try to follow the mandate of Islam to fight intolerance and oppression, whether against Muslims or any other group. His view is that Muslims are being oppressed in India, the Middle East, Bosnia, and other trouble spots and that oppression leads to fanaticism by a small minority. What is true is that extreme statements are much more likely to make the news. Moderate expressions are not likely to be seen on your television set or in your newspaper, even though there is a great need to see and hear them. But even if Islamic expert Graham Fuller is correct, views of greater tolerance can be nurtured by those of us in the West moving into genuine dialogue. Fuller adds: "Few Muslims around the world want to inflict endless punishment on the United States or go to war with it. Most of them recognize what happened on September 11 as a monstrous crime. . . . Muslim societies have multiple problems, but hating American political values is not among them. U.S. policymakers would be wise to drop this simplistic, inaccurate, and self-serving description of the problem." What is uncomfortably true, however, is that around the world, while most people deplored the brutal attack, at the same time many—particularly in the Muslim world—found a little satisfaction in "knocking down a notch or two arrogant U.S. leadership," as one reporter covering the Middle East phrased it in a conversation with me. A Gallup poll taken three months after the September 11 attack, among Muslims in six nations, found most of them condemning the action but only 18 percent believed that Arabs were involved in the attack. In Kuwait, 89 percent did not believe that Arabs were the perpetrators; in Pakistan, the figure was 86 percent; and in Indonesia, 74 percent.[46]

Incidents, large and small, can evoke the best in us or the worst in us. The Israeli-Palestinian struggle has brought to the surface a virulent anti-Semitism in Europe, and I have heard a little of it in conversations here in the United States. People don't have to agree with Israeli policy to avoid being anti-Semitic, but international action sometimes brings to the surface what is a latent hostility. Likewise, the legal and sexual difficulties in which less than 1 percent of Roman Catholic priests have enmeshed themselves become a convenient cover to anti-Catholicism by some. Seven months after the tragedy of September 11, local clergy of various faiths gathered in Brooklyn, and Naeem Baig, a Muslim leader, observed: "Sometimes we feel as Muslims that some people were looking for an opportunity to attack Islam, and they got one, and they are using it to the best. . . . Now the whole press is attacking Catholicism. Right now you look at any priest, and the first thing that comes to mind is, is something wrong with him or not. As Muslims we feel the same way. People are staring at me and they are thinking I am some terrorist. We told [the Catholic leaders], we understand what you are going through."[47]

Using religion as a cover for hatred is nothing new. Seventeenth-century French mathematician and philosopher Blaise Pascal observed, "Men never do evil so completely and cheerfully as when they do it from religious conviction."[48] Militancy in the Islamic community appears to be on the rise. People like prominent Muslim scholar Nurcholish Madjid of Indonesia, who preaches tolerance and understanding of other faiths, seem bland to young firebrands, many of whom had to leave their native countries because of their religious militancy. A *Washington Post* reporter in London visited mosques and Muslim bookstores and concluded that "militancy and intolerance have already won the high ground here."[49] When she asked the cashier at a bookstore why they carried so much material advocating violence, he responded: "Because it's part of the religion. You have to fight. Isn't that what the Christians believe?" In the midst of the Hindu-Muslim violent clashes in India and Pakistan, I took a taxi in Chicago. The driver, of Pakistani background, had limited command of English but commented, "Religion people. They crazy." Changing attitudes in people of any faith will not happen quickly. Leadership that appeals to the noble in us is essential. Genuine dialogue, which all too rarely takes place, can provide great assistance. Hatred, like a weed, can grow quickly; understanding, like an oak tree, takes more time, but it is magnificent when it matures.

The literal translation of *Islam* is "submission to the will of God," and for *Muslim*, a person "who surrenders to the will of God."[50] While over the centuries there have been terrible brutalities committed by Christians and Muslims against each other, all of history is not that negative. One example: "When the Najran Christians sent a delegation to Muhammad in Medina, they were well received. He offered them his mosque to hold their service. His relations with Christian Ethiopia were equally good. When the persecution of his followers in Mecca became unbearable, he sent them to Ethiopia. The negus, as the Ethiopian king was called, believed in their insistence on kinship with Christianity and protected them."[51] There have been enough positive developments in relations—though far too few—that in 1995 a book appeared with the title *Christians and Muslims: From Double Standards to Mutual Understanding*.[52] Unfortunately, the scars from wounds of the past have meant *very limited* mutual understanding. We have moved from the point where a seventh-century Christian described Muslims as "wild and untamed beasts who have merely the shape of human form."[53] Muslims know the history of the Crusades, started as a result of a history-making sermon by Pope Urban II near the small French city of

LePuy, probably the most significant postbiblical sermon ever preached, in which he called on Christians to remove Muslims and other infidels from the Holy Land. There were eight Crusades; the first is described by historian Rollin Armour:

> The first stage of the Crusade was led by misguided fanatics . . . whose followers unleashed terrible violence and carnage as they journeyed to Palestine. . . . A self-appointed preacher named Peter the Hermit . . . bred among his followers a passion to kill infidels, and the first "infidels" they saw were Jews. . . . They set upon Jews, first in Lorraine and then in the Rhine Valley, looting, killing, burning homes and synagogues and sometimes forcing baptisms. . . . Their belief [was] that because Jews were led by demons, killing them would hasten the End of the Age. . . . On July 15 [1099] the crusaders breached Jerusalem's walls and entered it in victory. Once in the city, the crusaders massacred virtually every person they found, Muslim and Jew . . . sparing only a few of the city's leaders. The chroniclers claimed that blood ran in the streets ankle deep. As soon as the slaughter ended and while the streets were still clogged with the bodies of the slain, the knights gathered in the Church of the Holy Sepulcher for High Mass to give thanks for their victory.[54]

In contrast, the United States has been fortunate that our few key early leaders generally believed strongly in tolerance. After the constitution was ratified in 1789, a banquet held in Philadelphia to celebrate that action included a special table for Jews—then a small part of our population—at which they served food prepared according to Jewish dietary traditions. Our Constitution, which does not mention God, called for an unusual experiment: no established national religion. Most of our states had an established religion at least in name, but by 1833, that no longer existed. We gradually became one nation on this and other issues. Our early newspapers, when referring to our country, used the plural, "the United States *are* . . ." As the consensus on religion and other issues changed, the verb changed to "the United States *is* . . ." In 1813, John Adams wrote to his one-time adversary Thomas Jefferson: "Checks and balances . . . are our only Security. . . . Every Species of Christians would persecute Deists, as either sect would persecute another if it had unchecked and unbalanced Power. . . . The Deists would persecute Christians, and Atheists would persecute Deists, with an unrelenting Cruelty, as any Christians would persecute them or one another."[55]

Despite our constitutionally mandated tolerant beginnings, you do not need to look at religious riots in India or clashes in the Middle East to find violent acts of intolerance. Religion historian Martin Marty notes that during World War II, the Jehovah's Witnesses circulated a pamphlet, "Reasons Why a True Follower of Jesus Christ Cannot Salute a Flag," because they believed (and believe) it is a form of idolatry. Citizens responded out of patriotic fervor or religious fanaticism by castrating a Witness member in Nebraska, tar and feathering an adherent in Wyoming, beating six of the Witnesses in Maine, and responding with other acts of violence around the nation, often with the police looking the other way.[56]

In 1929, comedian-philosopher Will Rogers wrote: "People talk peace, but men give their life's work to war. It won't stop till there is as much brains and scientific study put to aid peace as there is to promote war."[57] Who *should* lead such an endeavor? Who can still dream? I hope this portion of my book appeals to the idealism of those who should lead.

The suggestions for specific action made in earlier pages in this chapter may seem obvious, but the obvious too often is not taking place. Perhaps 1 percent of faith congregations are attempting to influence policy—and that may be a high figure. Not many more than that are reaching out to people with strongly differing beliefs. If we could get both of those figures to 5 percent, it would change our nation and our world. There are 350,000 houses of worship in the United States. Five percent of that figure would be 17,500. What a huge influence 17,500 congregations could have! In his classic, *Bowling Alone*, Robert Putnam writes:

> It is hard to see how we could redress the erosion [of cohesive activities] of the last several decades without a major religious contribution. . . . The First Amendment strictures have enabled us to combine unparalleled religiosity and denominational pluralism with a minimum of religious warfare. . . . Religion has played a major role in every period of civic revival in American history. So I challenge America's clergy, lay leaders, theologians, and ordinary worshipers: Let us spur a new, pluralistic, socially responsible "great awakening," so that by 2010 Americans will be more deeply engaged than we are today in one or another spiritual community . . . while at the same time becoming more tolerant of the faiths and practices of other Americans.[58]

Religion can be a powerful tool to lift us from the quicksand of indifference. That requires religious leaders to lead, to do more than pander. A study of inner-city churches that are responding to needs in their communities found a mean monthly expenditure of $691 per congregation on social needs.[59] The prophet Micah wrote, "What does the Lord require of you? To act justly and to love mercy and to walk humbly with your God."[60] Of these three *requirements*, the first two are generally ignored. And there are those who say, if the first two are ignored, the third becomes a pretense rather than a reality.

In 1963, Martin Luther King wrote:

> Darkness cannot drive out darkness
> Only light can do that.
> Hate cannot drive out hate;
> Only love can do that.

Hate multiplies hate,
Violence multiplies violence.
And toughness multiplies toughness
In a descending spiral of destruction.
The chain reaction of evil—
hate begetting hate,
wars producing more wars—
must be broken,
or we shall be plunged
into the darkness of annihilation.[61]

4

Pandering in Education

[That] our children lag behind their international peers strikes me as a bigger long-term threat to our national security than the rate of taxation paid on multimillion-dollar estates.

—Senator James Jeffords,
My Declaration of Independence (2001)

Officeholders are so cowed from getting out front on [education] issues and offering innovative, bold, and costly solutions that they are impotent to act even when the need is incredibly apparent.

—Joe Foote, Arizona State University, June 2002

Education Drift or Education Lift?

People in every field tend to "get into a rut" unless something forces change, and education is no exception. The security and economic well-being of the nation are being weakened by all of us—administrators, teachers, parents, and citizens—living too comfortably with superficial pleasantries. The education and legislative leaders who should awaken us to realities generally aren't doing it. Our deficiencies are compounded when knowledgeable people, who understand the improvements we need, are so mesmerized by day-to-day duties that they ignore long-range demands, and the inattention is frequently further compounded by lack of courage.

People from many nations look at our system of higher education—particularly the greater access for all students—and take some of its strengths and apply them, at least in part, to their own systems. At the graduate level, American higher education clearly leads the world. Students from virtually all nations head here because of that leadership. But no one, to my knowledge, is copying any significant part of our elementary and high school programs. A few schools abroad have tried to include some of the informality that is part of our system, compared to the generally much more vigorous discipline in the education systems of other nations, but not much beyond that is being copied—and many of our educators would like to see in our schools the greater discipline that is the one of the hallmarks of schools in other nations.

Much has been written about our deficiencies in science and math. I don't need to add to the healthy attention already given to these areas. However, sometimes they are treated as isolated exceptions to a general picture that is sound. There is much that is good about the U.S. education picture, but we have need for significant enrichment. Let me outline a few much-needed changes.

School Calendar

In Singapore, elementary and secondary students attend school 280 days a year, in Japan 243, and in Germany 240. In my state of Illinois, it is 176, with most states hovering around that figure; Maryland tops the list at 184. The average is slightly less than 180 days. Can our students learn as much in 180 days as the Germans do in 240? To ask the question is to answer it. Why do we go 180 days? In theory, so that our children can help to harvest the crops. Recently, I spoke to a university class of 270 in rural Illinois and asked how many had spent the last summer helping to harvest crops. One hand went up—and that surprised me; usually no hands are raised.

The National Education Commission on Time and Learning in 1994 reported significant deficiencies in our schools. In a revision and update of that report six years later, Dennis Doyle, a member of the commission, writes: "We know that American students spend too little time learning compared to many students overseas. German and Japanese youngsters, for example, in four years of what we would call high school, experience more than 3,300 hours of academic learning. . . . In contrast, the typical American [high school] student has about 1,800 hours of academic exposure. . . . We now know that time is the key learning variable—not intelligence, not curriculum, not standards, but time."[1] That typical U.S. high school student spends more time during a year watching television than in a classroom. The original report notes, "Our time-bound mentality has fooled us into believing that schools can educate all of the people all of the time in a school year of 180 six-hour days."[2]

By the time a student finishes secondary school in Japan, he or she has attended class as much as the average college student receiving a bachelor's degree in the United States—and that does not count the two to three hours a day of "cram schools" that follow the regular school day, which are designed to assist Japanese students to pass the rigorous exam that determines whether they will go to college, and if so, which one they may attend. If we increased attendance from 180 days to 210—a one-sixth increase—by the time a student finished the twelfth grade, that would be the equivalent of adding two additional years of schooling.

The U.S. Commissioner of Education complained in 1894 that the shorter school calendar was

> a distinct loss this year, the average number of days of school having been reduced from 193.5 to 191. . . . The constant tendency [has been] toward a reduction of time. First, the Saturday morning session was discontinued; then the summer vacations were lengthened; the morning sessions were shortened; the afternoon sessions were curtailed; new holidays were introduced. . . . The boy of today must attend 11.1 years in order to receive as much instruction . . . as the boy of fifty years ago received in eight years. . . . It is scarcely necessary to look further than this for the explanation for the greater amount of work accomplished . . . in the German and French schools.[3]

The Beacon schools of Oakland, California, prekindergarten through high school, are privately financed. Before high school, students attend 240 days a year, and in high school, 210. When asked why, a school official replied, "We are no longer living in an agricultural society, so there is no need to try to fit everything into 180 days."[4] Families are permitted to take children out of school for family vacations at any time during the school year. Every six weeks, two or more teachers take time off for vacation or study. Trained teachers who serve full-time in the school take their place. Substitute teachers are not used. Classes are small, and the school's specialties include the arts and technology. The founder, Thelma Farley, taught in traditional public schools for twenty years and found herself saying over and over, "Somehow this isn't working." But it is at Beacon schools. Students enter with low standardized scores, sometimes severely low scores. They are tested between the fourth and fifth grades and each year after that, through the eighth grade. After a short time, they consistently test two levels above their grade in both math and reading.[5]

What is frequently called "year-round schooling" sometimes refers to an increase in the number of days, sometimes simply to an altered school calendar of 45 days of schooling and 15 days off, and sometimes to voluntary two-week periods of school—usually called *intersessions*—during what had been the summer vacation, often with a special emphasis such as civics (an almost forgotten word) or math or environmental studies. There are additional variations in the school calendar, but these are the basic three. They have the following in common:

- The initial reaction by teachers and parents may be hostile if the change is not carefully planned.
- Teachers will have to be paid more, and many schools will have to be air-conditioned, the additional cost factor causing a little public concern. (Totally aside from the length of the school year, we do not help teacher quality by giving low pay. A teacher with a master's degree earns $23,000 a year less on average than someone in another field with a master's degree.)[6] One of the advantages of a longer school year is that teachers are paid more. If I want to improve my home, I will have to sacrifice a little, and if we want to improve our nation's schools, we will have to sacrifice a little.
- Where it is handled well, there may be initial skepticism on the part of many, but soon teachers, parents, and administrators come to like it. Many schools with additional days or a differing schedule than the traditional one find they have a waiting list for teachers who want to be employed, while neighboring districts have a hard time getting good teachers.

The real way to judge whether the longer school calendar is an improvement: the results. In most instances, they are clearly positive but not spectacular. People who seek dramatic changes are not likely to find them in this change or in other modifications. All students do not show improved scores or learning habits, judging by the tests, but most do. Here is a fairly typical situation: Bardstown, Kentucky, has a school district with above-average poverty. They have had year-round school sessions for five years. Since the inauguration of the program, the dropout rate has lowered from 4.5 percent to 2.7 percent; grades of A's and B's grew from 56.5 percent to 58.2 percent; ACT scores went from an average of 19.1 to 19.7; the percentage of the senior class attending college increased from 62 percent to 74 percent; and disciplinary referrals dropped 16.1 percent. Spectacular? No. Solid improvement? Yes. It would be interesting to follow that senior class for ten years and compare their experiences, earnings, divorce rate, and other gauges with a similar class before Bardstown changed the school calendar.

Additional days in school are not a substitute for quality teaching. Nor are they a substitute for having a home atmosphere that encourages intellectual growth. But they can help. One study concludes: "Year-round schooling at the secondary level is often associated with an increase in the number of graduation credits attained as well as a decrease in dropout rates. At the elementary level a positive impact on student achievement is well documented. . . . There is compelling evidence that the positive academic effects of year-round schooling are enhanced for at-risk students."[7] When school administrators who changed their school calendar were surveyed about various options, not a single administrator preferred the traditional calendar that most schools use today.

These preferences are based on solid numbers. The San Diego Unified School District's Academic Performance Index from 1999 to 2001 found the average growth in all 118 elementary schools' scores to be 44.90, while the average growth for the 49 schools with the altered calendar increased 60.48. Fourteen of the 118 schools regressed and only one with the year-round calendar.[8]

Another study by academicians at the University of Missouri and Tennessee State University noted that during the long summer vacation of the traditional school year, scores for all students in mathematics declined. However, in reading, middle- and upper-income students did not score lower, but children from poor families showed a decline. Undoubtedly, in the families with greater income there is more reading, more newspapers and magazines, more books, and more opportunity for children to practice and enhance their reading skills. This study concluded, "Educational policymakers could simply choose to live with the diminished learning opportunities and decay in skills that accompany the present dominant school calendar."[9] Or they can change things and help their students.

Because of the mobility of students, and because of the differing quality in teaching, results are never identical, but the trend is generally clear. A report on two schools in Durham, North Carolina, is perhaps typical: "The Year Round Schools at School A and School B, in their first year of operation, have had a significant positive effect on the achievement of students at these two schools. Students at School A outperformed the expected gains in reading (4.4 points versus the expected 4 scale points) and in math (7.2 points versus the expected 6 points). Students at School B also made impressive gains in reading (4.3 versus the expected 4 points) and math (8.6 points versus the expected 6 points)."[10]

Minority students appear to be among the principal beneficiaries of the altered calendar. Two researchers from Johns Hopkins University followed 790 students for sixteen years to measure the loss, if any, from the summer vacation period. One of their conclusions: "Children in Baltimore's poor neighborhoods were learning at the same rate as middle-class students during the school year but fell much further behind during the summer.

Children from more affluent families tended to enroll in summer camps, music or art lessons and were encouraged to attack summer reading lists. Poorer children had less to do in the summer and tended to forget more of what they learned during the previous year."[11] *USA Today* reported a survey of teachers about the time it takes to renew reading skills after the summer break. Among the teachers, 3 percent said it took one to two weeks, 38 percent two to four weeks, 45 percent more than a month, and 12 percent more than two months.[12]

The National Education Commission on Time and Learning reported these advantages to year-round schools:

- reduced summer learning loss
- quicker diagnosis and intervention of student learning problems
- higher student attendance
- higher teacher attendance and fewer substitute days
- fewer dropouts
- reduced in-school vandalism
- fewer discipline referrals[13]

And here is a report on one school:

> Test scores continue to climb at Congress Extended Year-Round School in Milwaukee, Wisconsin. . . .
>
> Mrs. Mary Beth Minkley, principal of Congress Elementary and Early Childhood Center . . . led the effort to change the calendar in 1996. . . . At Congress, school begins on the last Thursday in July, has only a four-week summer break, and has extended the number of instructional days from the usual 180 to 196.
>
> But those are not the only changes that have led to Congress's success. Volunteer hours at the school last year totaled over 15,000. A School Governance Council meets monthly. . . . Congress is a Title I school with about 83 per-

> cent of all students qualifying for free or reduced cost meals. Congress enrolls close to 700 students ranging in age from 6 weeks through grade 5.
>
> Test scores on the Wisconsin Knowledge and Concepts Examination, Grade 4, are consistently higher than district scores. Over the three years that the new calendar has been in effect, most test scores have tripled in the areas of reading, math, science, social studies and language. Compared to students throughout the district, Congress students outperform those at other schools in each area, from 3 percent in social studies all the way to 20 percent higher in math scores. . . . Six more schools in the Milwaukee area have adopted year-round calendars since the start of year-round at Congress.[14]

Other schools have started down a path of change by offering two weeks of special study on a particular topic and then gradually adding additional two-week periods on differing topics. It is a relatively noncontroversial way to ease into a longer school year. A few have self-financed this by charging a small tuition, which is not ideal because families with limited income are excluded, but it is a way to start a program with little controversy. I have spoken to teachers' institutes and meetings of school administrators about the idea, and I have received a warm, though sometimes not enthusiastic, response after the concept is carefully explained.

Critics of the concept cite schools that formerly opened after Labor Day and note that when they open earlier, for the first few days attendance is diminished. Also, a few schools that started the idea dropped it, apparently because its introduction had not been carefully and sensitively planned. California now has 1,605 school districts with a differing schedule, and all but five states (Delaware, Maine, New Hampshire, Rhode Island, and Vermont) have at least one school district that has adopted a changed calendar. Enrollment in these public schools (many private schools also have it) has gone from 362,000 in the 1986–87 school year to 2,184,000 in 2001–2.

What is the barrier to this improvement in our educational system? As one opponent of the idea writes, "If year-round education is such a proven concept, why after 80-plus years do only 3 percent of the nation's schools have such a calendar?"[15] For those who look for a single magic bullet that will dramatically elevate test scores, the results are not spectacular enough. A scattering of schools, notably in California, have had a modified calendar for more than thirty years. If anyone were to suggest to those districts going back to the more typical U.S. school calendar, it would cause great controversy. Summer school as a penalty, only for those who fail, is not an unqualified success. In 2000 in New York City, 35,000 students received mandates to attend summer school because of failing grades. Almost 14,000 did not show up. And among those who did, only 57 percent passed—yet that is almost 12,000 who did pass, certainly not a total loss for New York City's schools.[16] However, the biggest barrier is not the lack of results but the lack of courage. Not wanting to offend parents or teachers or taxpayers, even "leaders" who know this step will help are too often meekly quiet.

The camping and tourism industries also oppose the change, for obvious reasons, and frequently, the immediate, emotional response to the idea is negative, particularly from teachers and parents, if it is not properly explained and planned. If an elementary school modifies its calendar but the high school in an area does not, there are complaints from a few parents who have difficulty coordinating their summer vacation plans. Texas has actually experienced a decline in the number of changed calendar schools because of impediments to the idea placed by the Dallas school district and the State of Texas. However, advocates claim that nationally, less than 1 percent of the schools that shift to the new calendar eventually change back.[17] What is clear from the research data is that a changed calendar, even if it does not add days but calls for shorter vacation periods (e.g., 45 days of attendance, 15 days of vacation), has a positive impact on most, but not all, students' test scores. The status quo is often more comfortable than change, for teachers and administrators and parents. As one educator observed: "The status quo can stand on its own merit, even when there isn't any."[18]

If you are looking for controversy-free ways of significantly improving education, this is not your option, but I should add, neither is anything else of which I'm aware. No one is offended if administrators continue to drift, and few challenge them to do better. Pandering is easy, leadership more difficult, and too many follow the easy path, a downhill road for our nation. Ascending this educational hill is more strenuous but also can be exhilarating.

If properly planned and handled, adding more days can enrich the curriculum in many ways. Retarding that enrichment in all schools somewhat are the too frequent mandates on educators for everything from driver's education to some legislator's favorite project. Basics then sometimes get ignored. Henry Kissinger tells of a problem he had in leading on foreign policy: The post–Cold War generation is "the product of an educational system that puts little emphasis on history [and] often lacks perspective about foreign affairs."[19] Enriching education in history and geography and the arts and other fields would help the nation.

The federal government could assist local schools by providing a small grant for each student who attends at least 210 days a year. The grant should be graduated, so that schools with a high percentage of economically disadvantaged (Title I) students receive more money than others.

Lloyd H. Elliott, the former president of George Washington University and a leader in all levels of education, wrote these thoughtful words:

> The days of an agrarian-based calendar—three months or more for children to help with the farm work—became outdated more than a century ago. . . .

> A longer school year should, in most school districts, also bring a broadened curriculum that will require a longer school day. In many schools, it is athletics that keep those who participate some eight or nine hours each day on the school grounds. Shouldn't we do as much for those who can benefit from similar programs in music, art, dance, theater, or other studies? . . .
>
> Without three months to disconnect from school, spend energies in less constructive activities, or break from all academic matters, fewer kids, we can hope, will join the gangs to peddle drugs and flout the laws. . . .
>
> Is the need really with us? Yes, there is the necessity for such a radical step. It is the explosion of knowledge. . . .
>
> Will we see adequate schools in the first quarter of this new century? Can the most powerful nation in the world—and the richest—allocate a fraction of that wealth in order to have schools good enough to service and protect its own leadership? Or do we sacrifice that leadership because we are too shortsighted to continue what we have so fortunately been given?
>
> It remains to be seen.[20]

The question for leaders today is more than, Can Johnny read? A more basic question: Can our students compete with the rest of the world? Our best students can, but far too many are not being adequately prepared. As with any other improvement, a better educational system will come only with sacrifice and hard work, from school administrators, teachers, parents, and students. But what is more important, convenience and longer vacations, or better education? It's easier to drift, easier to pander, than to alter our path.

Prekindergarten Education

In 1858, Oliver Wendell Holmes wrote, "A child's education should begin at least 100 years before he was born."[21] We cannot rework each child's heritage, but we can do much better than we are doing. We know that 81 percent of those in our prisons and jails are high school dropouts and that the sooner educational deficiencies or learning disabilities are detected, the less difficult it is to take constructive action. It is easier to partially remold a fourth grader than a tenth grader, and it is easier to improve opportunity when problems are detected at the age of four than in the fourth grade.

Albert Shanker, for many years the president of the American Federation of Teachers until his death robbed us of an important creative voice, told the story of a factory assembly line. During the course of putting a certain manufactured product together, 25 percent of the parts fell off before they got to the end of the line, and at the end of the assembly belt, another 25 percent were found to be defective. If you ran the factory, you would recognize that you had a problem and try to fix it. He likened that assembly line to education.

There is no simple, single answer to improving that assembly line, but there is ample evidence that preschool education is one piece important for improvement. It is not a lone answer that can be used in isolation from the educational deficiencies of the parents. But it can provide substantial assistance and really make a difference. The Albert Shanker Institute operated by the American Federation of Teachers has focused on this. So have others, including a thoughtful and innovative former business leader in Chicago, Irving Harris, who has used his resources to bring about change.

France has done as much or more than any nation in this field. Some call it "the crown jewel of the French system."[22] The French educational culture differs appreciably from ours, among other things, because it is a centralized system in which, for example, third graders throughout the nation are studying the same subject during the same week, so that if a student from Lyon transfers to a school in the northern part of France, the adjustment is primarily social and not academic. We are not likely ever to have a national prekindergarten program of great uniformity—but that can be good as well as bad, because we can profit by what works and what does not work.

The following are some features of France's preschool system:

- Teachers are highly qualified academically.
- Health screening is provided for all children.
- Special drop-in centers are available for mothers who don't work outside the home. Children must be at least eighteen months old, and mothers cannot leave their children here more than four half-days per week.
- Working mothers have different options, with French law encouraging them to take their children to licensed providers, who are required to undergo special training.
- At age three, preschool education begins.
- Roughly twice as much is spent nationally on prekindergarten education as in the United States.

While there is always a question about the reliability of comparing students in two differing cultures, the French results make clear that a universal prekindergarten program in the United States would lift our educational product.

France provides schooling for everyone starting at three years of age, Italy does so for 80 percent in that age bracket, Belgium, 95 percent, and Greece, 65 percent. In the United States, the rough estimate is that 30 percent of three-year-olds are receiving schooling or at least custodial care. When four-year-olds are included, many more nations are added to the list, including the United Kingdom, Luxembourg, Spain, and the Netherlands, which provide for almost all children in this age group. The United States hovers near 50 percent for four-year-olds.

The cost in France is $5,500 per student for the early years. That would spell huge expenditures in our country. Now the 30 percent who receive the education are overwhelmingly from middle- and upper-income families—those who need the help the least. The Head Start program is an exception to that.

We know enough about the brain to understand that those early years, even early months, are most important in children's development. That is true for their emotional health, which we do understand, but it is also true for their intellectual health, much less widely understood.

Newsweek highlighted a philosophical division on prekindergarten schooling: Should three- and four-year-olds only "have a good time" and in the process learn social skills or, say others, should they also be acquiring some feel for letters and numbers and how they sound and then how they look in print or on some blocks?[23] President George W. Bush comes down on the reading side. My belief is that he is correct, that without going so far as formal classes for three- and four-year-olds, there are games and other ways for children to learn about letters and numbers while also enjoying themselves and acquiring social skills. A study in Dallas, in an area where children scored in the bottom 1 percent of a national preschool test, showed that with such simple devices as name tags, the children learn basic reading skills. *Newsweek* noted, "By the end of third grade, 55 percent of the children who attended [the literacy-emphasis preschool] and a local elementary [school] with a strong literacy emphasis were reading at grade level, compared with 5 percent in the control group." The evidence is overwhelming that an enriching preschool program can make a great difference, particularly for children coming from low-income households.

Isabell Sawhill, a senior economist at the Brookings Institution, writes:

> Almost all experts now agree that a preschool experience . . . is one of the most effective strategies for improving later school performance. . . .
>
> Early interventions, especially with disadvantaged children, have produced a variety of positive results . . . [including] high school achievement, less retention in grade, a reduced need for special education at a later age, and less crime. . . . The best results come from programs that begin early, include children from the most disadvantaged homes, and provide intensive education and other services over a lengthy period.[24]

Would the program be costly? Yes. Sawhill places that at $18 billion a year—a great deal of money, but less than one-third of the increase in the defense budget requested by President Bush for FY 2003, not counting the cost of the war in Iraq. The other question: Is it costly *not* to do it? These costs are huge, and no one can calculate them precisely.

The more difficult question: Do we have the vision and the understanding and the courage to do it? Or are we going to take the easy route that will be so costly for our children and future generations? Here again, we must ask ourselves if it is not better to sacrifice now so that the future of our children will be improved and more secure.

Adult Literacy

The most conservative estimate is that at least twenty-three million adult Americans cannot read a newspaper and cannot fill out an employment form. About three million cannot recognize their name in block letters. That reduces the productivity of our nation, which is the key to our standard of living, and makes it more likely that some in this category will feel forced into a life of crime. But the biggest drawback to these numbers is that these adults are extremely limited in their ability to stimulate their children to read and cannot help them with their school work when they reach that age.

This huge deficiency relates directly to the controversies surrounding test scores in schools. While I know the weaknesses of testing—mobility of students and the greater emphasis on testing than learning—I still favor testing as a means of determining what is being taught, however crude it may be.

Let me show you what is true in my area of southern Illinois that can be duplicated in any region of the nation. Of the forty high schools in the rural, southern one-fifth of Illinois, the high school with the top score (67.4 percent of students meet or exceed state standards) is Carbondale Community High School, which spends $12,955 per student. Next to last is Cairo High School (where 14.6 percent of students meet or exceed state standards), with an expenditure of $14,078 per student—$1,123 more per student than Carbondale High School. The school with the second highest score, Steeleville High School (where 62.8 percent meet or exceed state standards), spends $9,099 per student, while dead last in scoring is Meridian High School (with scores slightly lower than Cairo's), which allocates $607 more per student than the second-highest ranking school.[25]

What do the bottom two schools have in common? A high percentage of the families in those two districts are poor. A survey would find a low average educational attainment by the parents, parents who cannot help their children with their school work. The most important contribution that could be made in those two districts is a massive assault on adult illiteracy and near-illiteracy. That would reduce the poverty level, but much more important, it would also provide for a better future for the children of those adults.

I do not suggest—nor do the statistics—that the amount spent on education is unimportant. But that is less important than the education attainment level of the parents. Where you have an unusual combination of strong leadership and dedicated teachers, that pattern of bad scores by children of poorly educated parents can be broken, Earhart Elementary School in Chicago being an example, but that is an unusual exception to the general pattern.[26]

The message is clear: To *really* raise test scores among students, we should do what we can right now as early in their childhood as possible, but we must also reach their parents. We have inched ahead on adult basic education but only a little. I was chief sponsor of the National Literacy Act, and I had as my goal virtually ending illiteracy in this nation by the year 2000. My bill passed, but I regret to say we are a long way from that goal. It is a peripheral issue with administrators and policy makers, and it really needs the leadership of a president who goes on television, explains how this problem is harming the nation, and then enlists schools, religious agencies, civic groups, welfare leaders, governors, and many others in this cause. Cuba claims that President Fidel Castro has lowered adult illiteracy from 83 percent to 3 percent. Those figures may be exaggerated, but in Cuba and in a few other developing nations, there have been dramatic improvements. We need dramatic changes in the developing nation within our country.

While presidential leadership is the ideal answer, I have seen local schools and small counties take this on and make real progress. The key is always one person who is motivated to lead. Before I left the Senate, I visited eighteen schools on the West Side and South Side of Chicago, the poorer areas of the city. I took no reporters with me. Overall, the schools were better than I had anticipated, with some stark deficiencies. School libraries frequently had mostly empty shelves, not books; some workbooks for students had old pencil markings from the previous year with the right or wrong answers, erased but still clearly visible to current students. In one school, within five minutes after I arrived, the principal said, "These students don't have much potential." I sensed how her attitude permeated everything and everyone. At another school in a dismal neighborhood, I walked in expecting to be depressed and instead found that the principal, Dr. Arletta Holloway, an African American, had the students and the teachers excited about what they were doing. She brought in parents who could not read and write and had volunteers teach them the basics; she had other parents volunteering for special duties. People had an enthusiasm for their work as students, teachers, or parents that was contagious. One leader did it.

In the case of adult literacy, the barriers are indifference by most of us and hidden embarrassment by the adults who need help. For leaders, the comfortable status quo is easier than bestirring themselves to become an Arletta Holloway or her counterpart on a school board, or a state legislator, or a governor.

The best answer, as I said before, would be for the president to go on national television and make an appeal to schools, civic groups, religious organizations, and others to massively assault this huge, hidden problem in our nation because it could mean so much in the lives of adult Americans and even more in the lives of their children. We could, like Cuba claims it has done, stamp out illiteracy in a generation or even a decade, if it became a national priority. The federal government, states, counties, local libraries, school districts, and community colleges, as well as voluntary organizations, could all be part of a unified effort that would enrich this nation immensely. But that means shaking up the comfortable status quo. It requires leading, not ignoring this basic problem. Pandering has to be replaced by initiative. It will take a few dollars to get this done, but not many. The returns on this investment are almost immediate.

Foreign Languages

We are the only nation in which people can go through grade school, high school, attend four years of college, get a Ph.D.—and never have a year of foreign language instruction. So far as

I can determine, we are the only nation in which you can go through the elementary grades and not study another language. That costs us now in lost jobs from international sales, in security, in cultural enrichment, and it suggests a lack of sensitivity to the other 96 percent of the world's population.

In television listings for April 15, 1992, the lightweight boxing match between Angel Hernandez and Sera Anunciado received top billing. To the embarrassment of many, they quickly learned that *Sera Anunciado* means "to be announced" in Spanish. In a country with so many citizens of Hispanic descent, mistakes of this nature are embarrassing.

And there are many other problems. For example, consider the heading on an item in the *New York Times:* "U.S. Gets Too Few U.N. Jobs, Report Says."[27] The story quotes the chair of the House Committee on International Relations, Rep. Henry Hyde, saying that having more Americans in UN jobs at all levels would give us "a greater stake in the operation and success of the international body." He is correct. What the story does not say is that a major problem that hinders more Americans from obtaining key jobs is lack of language skills.

Our apparent disinterest in communicating with others in their own language hinders our growth and often leads to misunderstandings and confusion, both within and beyond our borders. Four months after the September 11 tragedy, columnist Thomas Friedman wrote: "What produced this iron curtain of mistrust and misunderstanding [between the United States and the Arab world]? . . . One is our own failure over the past two decades to really explain ourselves *in Arabic* and to puncture canards about U.S. policy with hard facts. The Bush team has yet to provide a dossier, *in Arabic*, detailing all the evidence against bin Laden" (my emphasis).[28]

After September 11, the FBI and the CIA scrambled to find people with Arabic language skills. The lack of sophistication in this field is illustrated by one applicant's experience:

> Less than a week after the attacks on the World Trade Center and the Pentagon, I responded to the FBI's calls for Arabic translators. I know of a half-dozen other Middle Eastern studies graduates who also applied—Ph.D.s who, like me, are proficient in one or more Arabic dialects, as well as in Modern Standard Arabic. Ultimately—dismayed by what seemed to be the agency's flawed understanding of what proficiency in Arabic means—none of us pursued our candidacies.
>
> I applied less than a week after September 11 but wasn't called for the four-and-a-half hour translation test until January. It wasn't until February that I sat for a four-hour interview and polygraph test. . . . The slow pace, however, wasn't the most unsettling characteristic of the process. . . . The FBI's Arabic translation test simply does not measure all the language skills needed for intelligence gathering focused on Arabic speakers.
>
> The Arabic language test . . . was solely in Modern Standard Arabic, the Arabic most frequently studied at American universities. This is the form used for official speeches and in the news media in Arab countries—but almost never in conversation. . . . A non-native speaker who learned only Modern Standard Arabic would not be able to understand Arabic speakers talking to one another.[29]

We do not understand what it takes to effectively communicate with speakers of Arabic, and this prevents us from better understanding their culture, beliefs, and traditions and from seeing them as individuals with desires and needs similar to our own.

An interesting experiment took place among 700 first, second, and third grade Jewish and Arab students in Israel. The Arabs were taught Hebrew and the Jews Arabic. Stereotypes diminished. Attitudes changed. For example, "Among the Arabs, the higher the proficiency in Hebrew, the higher were the attitudes toward peace in the Middle East."[30] And Jewish students in Tel Aviv who studied Arabic and learned conversational Arabic showed "improved attitudes toward Arabs, willingness to get to know Arabs on a personal level, [and] willingness to learn Arabic to become friends with Arabs."[31] The greatest barrier to peace anywhere in the world is the lack of understanding, and removing the language part of that barrier can be significantly helpful. The lesson from this for us is clear: Exposure to another language also makes us more sensitive to those outside our borders. We need that sensitivity. It is easy to blame Congress and an administration for our anemic record on foreign economic assistance, but that policy emerges from an insensitive and unaware people. When I studied foreign languages many years ago, we learned nothing about other cultures as we memorized words and learned to conjugate verbs. Today, language learning is vastly different and better with growth in understanding other cultures. But we need to offer these learning opportunities to more students more consistently.

I once spent a night in a tent in the Sahara at the suggestion of my friend Congressman Stephen Solarz, learning about the problems of the people in what was called the Spanish Sahara. In addition to hearing about their yearning for independence from Morocco, I visited a primitive school (only for boys) in a battered tent in which there were no textbooks, only a small blackboard and chalk—and these students, whose native tongue is Arabic, were learning Spanish. How ironic, I thought, that if they were in a grade school in the United States, they would have desks and books and pencils and electric lights and school lunches and many things these boys do not even dream of—yet these young people in this primitive setting are acquiring foreign language skills that most U.S. elementary school students are not taught.

Research shows that acquiring another language early in life is easier, among other reasons, because young children are not embarrassed to make mistakes as they acquire a language and because they use all their senses in learning another tongue. The older we are, the more likely we are to be trying to acquire another language while seated. When a small boy or girl says, "Throw the ball," there is a greater likelihood that he or she will be actually throwing the ball, learning with all the senses. An adult is sitting at a desk reciting, "Throw the ball," and all the senses are not being used.

A century ago, all college students took a foreign language or Latin, and most high school students did. Then during World War I, an emotional anti–foreign language binge hit the nation, particularly in opposition to the teaching of German, and grade schools, high schools, and colleges in large numbers dropped foreign languages from the curriculum. In the midst of the foreign language hysteria, *Baltimore Sun* columnist H. L. Mencken wrote tongue-in-cheek in one of his columns that he supported the public mood: "If English was good enough for Jesus Christ, it's good enough for me." Many churches that served immigrants awkwardly shifted to English. Decades later, during the Vietnam War, students had sit-ins at university administration offices and sometimes engaged in acts of violence, such as burning buildings. Almost unnoticed in the midst of more graphic confrontations was the student demand that many requirements be dropped from the curriculum. Deleting a foreign language mandate seemed to be an easy thing for a college administration. It is one of the invisible costs of the Vietnam War.

Yale University awarded its first three Ph.D.'s in 1860 "to enable us to retain in this country many young men . . . who now resort to German universities for advantages of study."[32] The following year, a doctoral dissertation at Yale was written in Latin. All schools required foreign language capability for this advanced degree. The University of Chicago mandated reading ability in two foreign languages to get a doctorate. So did others. Even with these requirements, William James, a professor at Harvard who pioneered in psychology as well as philosophy and who had no doctorate, expressed concern that in 1903 the nation produced 337 Ph.D.'s and seemed to be heading toward a "doctor-monopoly in teaching," along with lower standards.[33] Since then, the academic standards to get the doctorate have declined—particularly in requiring foreign languages for all doctorates—but the demand for the doctorate, particularly in second-tier institutions, has escalated. In a world that needs greater international sensitivity, too many teachers and schools are not providing it. The undergraduate school of Columbia University in New York City is called Columbia College. That undergraduate school has a requirement that before a student can receive a bachelor's degree he or she must pass a course in swimming—but fortunately, there is now also a requirement for foreign language instruction.[34]

However, there is growing awareness that we are depriving our students of something they will need. Louisiana has mandated foreign languages in grades four through eight and has seven school districts with French and Spanish immersion programs. As I write this in 2002, approximately 7 percent of the nation's elementary school students receive at least a little foreign language exposure. That's not good, but it's better than the 1 percent of twenty years ago. That still leaves 93 percent of our elementary school students culturally impoverished. At higher levels of education, there is progress, but not much. There is a slowly increasing number of colleges and universities requiring foreign language study, but the need grows much more rapidly than our recognition of the need.

Elementary schools are where we should begin foreign language study and then follow through at all levels. The earlier we acquire foreign language skills, the better. People at the age of ninety can acquire a foreign language, but the evidence multiplies that the earlier we are exposed to another language, the more quickly it is acquired and the greater the likelihood of *thinking* in another language as well as *speaking* in it.

What stops us? School boards, administrators, legislators, and others either believe it is unimportant or they recognize its importance but also recognize that it will cost a little to move in this direction. That takes courage. Decision makers may have to face parents who say, "I didn't waste my time studying foreign languages, and I did all right." Anything that might be difficult for Johnny or Jane may run into resistance, if educating the public on the issue does not take place first. The irrational anti-immigrant sentiment may play a role. "I want my children to have American ideas, not foreign ideas," some may say who see language instruction as somehow caving in to the immigrant population. A good foreign language program will cost a few dollars; bowing to those who would squander money on other things rather than invest in the future is deceptively attractive. It is easier, more comfortable, to lean on excuses than to admit we're hurting our children.

Study Abroad

For the 2002–3 school year, 584,000 international students studied in colleges and universities in the United States. That's good for them and good for us. But only slightly more than 1 percent of our students study abroad, and two-thirds of them enroll in western Europe. That's better than not studying abroad, but 95 percent of the world's population growth in the next fifty years will take place in the developing world, and it is important that we understand the people of those regions better and they understand us better. Parents, teachers, and college administrators should put greater stress on study abroad, and the federal government should do the same. Excellent programs like the Fulbright exchanges have gradually been shrinking while the federal budget grows. That makes no sense.

It's politically easy to cut programs that send U.S. students and faculty abroad or bring others to our shores. But we're making a grave mistake in allowing this to happen. Students who study abroad eventually will be our leaders and much better leaders for having had this chance. The Senate and the nation have benefited substantially from the learning experience of Senator Chris Dodd of Connecticut during his service in Latin America in the Peace Corps. What if one or two members of the House or Senate had served in the Vietnam area or attended school in that region for one year? Maybe we would not have had that huge and unnecessary loss of life. Fourteen years after Lyndon Johnson stepped down as president, Senator William Fulbright reflected, "I'm sure that President Johnson would never have pursued the war in Vietnam if he'd ever had a Fulbright [scholarship] to Japan, or say Bangkok, or had any feeling for what these people are like and why they acted the way they did."[35]

Two-thirds of the students at St. Olaf College in Minnesota at some point study abroad. Kalamazoo College in Michigan and Grinnell College in Iowa also have good records. "They're private schools," you might comment. That's true, and it makes it easier, but the University of Idaho is better in this respect than almost all other private or public colleges. Why should these fine schools be almost in isolation with such a program? If we were to take 1 percent of the defense budget—or slightly less than $4 billion—and use it for sending U.S. students abroad for a semester or a year, we would build a world of greater understanding, greater security, and fewer needless deaths.

The Rotary Clubs sponsor international high school students living for a school year in American homes or U.S. students living in other nations for a similar period. Who can ever calculate what good that has done? It is an immense contribution. This good work may be related to the fact that Rotary defies the general trend, outlined by Robert Putnam in *Bowling Alone*, of organizations that are steadily losing members. After reaching a plateau in growth, its membership is rising once again.

Henry Kissinger writes: "The problem is not the inadequacy of individual leaders but rather the systemic problem of their cultural preparation."[36] That "cultural preparation" can be enhanced by exchanges that benefit not only the immediate students but the many families and fellow students and others with whom they have a chance to relate.

A dramatically improved and enlarged exchange program would also help on another difficulty. The author of *Bowling Alone* states, "The average college graduate today knows little more about public affairs than did the average high school graduate in the 1940's."[37] Recharging our civic batteries is no simple task, but studying abroad gives students and faculty a chance to learn more about the rest of the world, and almost inevitably, that stimulates interest in our own government and its policies. That does not cure the nation's lack of civic engagement, but this medicine would help.

Higher Education

There is internal pandering within the higher education community and pandering by public officials and education leaders on much more sweeping issues that impact on our society.

The excessive use and abuse of academic jargon within the higher education community is an example of pandering internally, producing articles in isolated fields that meet the "publish or perish" criteria but are read by few and contribute as close to nothing as you can get. It is not only the time wasted in writing these almost unreadable articles for tenure, salary, and prestige purposes, this pandering also takes academicians—and inevitably their students—away from the real world. In the political science field, we end up with articles like this one in the *American Political Science Review:* "Convergence and Restricted Preference Maximizing under Simple Majority Rule: Results from a Computer Simulation of Committee Choice in Two-

Dimensional Space." If that title confuses you, the following paragraph should clarify things:

> The object of this study is to estimate the effects on outcome convergence of restrictions imposed on preference-maximizing committee members. From a set of committee members' ideal points in a preference space, the computer simulation generates a set of proposals adopted by majorities of the committee in a choice space. Quantitative estimates of the dispersion of ideal points and majority-adopted proposals are given by the two-dimensional variance of ideal points and proposals. For m observations (proposals or ideal points), the variance is computed as follows:
>
> $$V=\sum_{j=1}^{m} \frac{((X_j-\bar{X})^2+(Y_j-\bar{Y})^2)}{m},$$
>
> where (X_j, Y_j) are the coordinates in the two-dimensional space of individual observations, j, and $(\bar{X}, \bar{Y})$ are means of the distributions of observations.[38]

I could provide many other examples where academic specialists are trying to make a hard science out of something that is not a hard science.

At Princeton, Brandeis, and one or two other schools, a student does not major in political science but in politics. I like that. I called the American Political Science Association, asking one of their executives for the trend in those majoring in this field. She said it was a slight trend downward. I asked what she believed to be the cause. "I have seen no studies," she replied, "but the criticism we hear most frequently is that it's not practical." A survey of U.S. Senators about this academic specialty would show the same impression.

This tendency toward academic jargon that equals nothingness exists in many areas. Back in 1939, Allan Nevins, who won two Pulitzer Prizes for his work in history, wrote an article for *Saturday Review* that caused a literary storm. Titled "What's the Matter with History?" it asserted that writers in the field—typified by "Professor Dryasdust"—focus so much attention on small items in microscopic detail that the meaning and fascination of events was being lost. Professor Dryasdust is "a plodding mediocrity. . . . At long intervals he prints an unreadable paper in some learned periodical. He may once in a decade excrete a slender, highly specialized, and to everybody concerned quite exhausting monograph. Apart from this his literary production is confined to an occasional spiteful review of some real historian."[39] In 1996, the scholarly journal *Social Text* published an article by New York University physics professor Alan Sokal titled "Transgressing the Boundaries: Toward a Transformative Hermeneutics of Quantum Gravity."[40] On the day of its publication, he announced that it was a planned hoax, an article written to show how meaningless these things can be.

Some of the ideas I've discussed in this chapter are unpopular, but that doesn't mean that they would not work. There is much precedent for the enactment of once unpopular policies that eventually have been educationally beneficial.

The Serviceman's Readjustment Act of 1944—much better known as the GI Bill—afforded more than ten million veterans a chance to obtain advanced education. The American Legion must be given major credit for its enactment, a measure that made a huge difference in the lives of most of those veterans—who otherwise would not have gone to college—and it enriched this nation immeasurably. We would not have our high standard of living in the United States if the GI Bill had not been enacted.

Controversial at the time of its passage (like the Marshall Plan), we now look back on it with great pride and wonder how it could have been a cause of political conflict. While the American Legion pushed education legislation, the other veterans organizations wanted those who served to receive a cash bonus of up to $5,000 or other benefits, instead of the educational program—and the cash bonus had greater popularity.

On February 16, 1944, while the House and Senate committees studied what to do to assist those who would be discharged after World War II, the leaders of the Veterans of Foreign Wars, the Military Order of the Purple Heart, the Disabled American Veterans, and the Regular Veterans Association sent a letter to all members of Congress saying that the educational benefit suggested by the American Legion was "so broad in scope and potential cost that its enactment would . . . probably not only prevent any consideration of several other more equitable proposals . . . [it] might also jeopardize the entire structure of veteran benefits."[41] The head of the American Veterans Committee said that because of veteran apathy toward education, it "will never be useful to the great majority of veterans."[42] Progressive journalists like Marquis Childs opposed it. Harvard president James B. Conant found the GI Bill "distressing." He said it did not "distinguish between those who can profit most by advanced education and those who cannot." He favored a GI Bill for "a carefully selected number of returned veterans" and expressed concern that the veterans otherwise would be "flooding the facilities for advanced education."[43] A University of Chicago dean said, "What will we do with married students on the campus? How will we house them? . . . Will we be embarrassed by the prospects of babies and by their arrival?"[44] A Columbia University leader observed, "If there is a baby, college is almost out of the question for any reasonable man . . . [even with] sufficient outside income."[45] One of the most vigorous opponents of the GI Bill, the usually progressive Robert Hutchins, president of the University of Chicago, said the proposal "threatens to demoralize education and defraud the veteran. . . . To say that this is reckless of Congress is a generous understatement." He called it an "easy road to ruin" that is designed as "a substitute for a dole."[46] Three percent of the colleges announced they planned to "segregate veterans from other students" if the bill passed.[47] The chair of the House Veterans Committee, Congressman John Rankin of Mississippi, said he opposed the educational benefits because it would expose the veterans "to the tainted theories of sociologists." We would, he said, become a nation "overeducated and undertrained. . . . I would rather send my child to a red schoolhouse than to a Red school teacher."[48]

The Legion proposal for veterans included hospitalization benefits, up to $300 in mustering out pay, loans to buy homes or businesses, as well as education. But the education benefits, compared to the much larger bonus at discharge that some advocated, created the controversy, and when the conference committee met to work out differences between the House and the Senate, which requires that a majority of both Senators and House members approve the measure in order to send it to the two houses for final enactment, Congressman Rankin, a power in the House, opposed it, and the House conferees deadlocked with three favoring it and three opposing it. Absent was Congressman John Gibson of Georgia. The conferees could not agree, and on the night of June 9, 1944, they adjourned with the understanding they would have a final meeting the next morning at ten. If no position changed, the idea would die. Congressman Gibson favored it, and near midnight, supporters of the measure called him in Georgia, got him to go to an Air Force base in "a slashing thunderstorm" and from there by motorcycle escort at 90 miles per hour to the airport at Jacksonville, Florida, where the American Legion had a plane waiting for him. The next morning, he cast the decisive vote, and the nation got the GI Bill.[49]

An unusual alignment of conservatives and liberals opposed the measure or supported it. Many feared huge unemployment numbers as veterans came home, and they recalled the veterans' marches on Washington after World War I—only now, there were many more veterans. American Legion commander Harry

Colomery testified to a congressional committee that he saw troubles ahead. "Except for England, this is the only country where the men who wore uniforms did not overthrow the government on either side of the conflict."[50] Passage of this measure turned out to be the Legion's finest hour. A committee headed by former Illinois governor and Legion national commander John Stelle got Legion posts around the nation mobilized politically to support it. President Roosevelt expressed concern that without legislation, veterans would be in breadlines and selling apples, a refrain heard over and over. Congressman Hamilton Fish, a conservative foe of Roosevelt, said that if the veterans came home and had to sell apples, "we would have chaotic and revolutionary conditions in America."[51] Almost no one thought of the GI Bill's educational benefits as being a real lift to the nation.

When the president signed the veterans legislation, the front-page story in the *New York Times* did not mention the educational benefits in the package until the tenth paragraph. Literally no one expected it to be as significant as it became. More than two million veterans took advantage of the program in the first years after World War II, and eventually more than ten million did. Most projections were that 2 to 3 percent of veterans would use the educational benefits.

University of Wisconsin enrollment went from 9,000 to 18,000. Rutgers University enrollment went from 7,000 to 16,000. I remember the packed dormitories in the small liberal arts school I attended in Nebraska, Dana College, as well as the "temporary housing" for married veterans that lasted decades. The GI Bill changed our nation's culture. At Tuttle Creek High School in Pennsylvania, the number of male graduates who got bachelor's degrees jumped from 3 percent to 30 percent. That happened all over the nation.

It cost $5.5 billion over seven years—a great deal of money in an annual federal budget of less than $100 billion. That first GI Bill (and there have been somewhat pale imitations since) produced 450,000 engineers, 240,000 accountants, 238,000 teachers, 91,000 scientists, 67,000 physicians, 17,000 journalists, and untold numbers of dentists and members of the clergy and a mosaic of people who enriched the nation almost beyond belief.[52] Veterans, regardless of family income, received $50 a month "subsistence allowance" for four years, $75 if they had dependents, plus up to $500 for tuition—which was more than Harvard or any other college charged—including books, lab fees, and similar charges.

Those veterans, who so many schools feared, did well. Most of them would not have gone to college or a technical school. They lifted the standard of living of the nation and raised the educational expectations of their children and future generations. President Conant of Harvard, who had opposed the plan, called the veterans "the most mature and promising students Harvard has ever had."[53] Not one of Columbia University's 7,826 veterans "was in serious scholastic difficulty" as of April 1946.[54]

What lessons are there in this for us? One is the prudent use of resources. If our leaders had done the immediately popular thing and provided a cash bonus, it would have stimulated our economy a little, but the lasting benefits would be almost nonexistent. Congress clearly wanted to benefit the veterans and "please the folks back home," but at least some members looked at the long-term benefits.

Long-term needs today include building a more skilled work force. Every economic study suggests we must invest more in education or we will harm the nation. Former Labor Secretary William Brock, a Republican who had previously served as a senator from Tennessee, told a New York City audience, "Sixty nine percent of American businesses believe their growth may be impeded by an inability to find and employ individuals with the skills that are requisite to business needs."[55] We must be more demanding of students in traditional school settings, of those studying for a trade—and more demanding of our society, which sets their goals and sometimes limits their potential. For *their* future, for *our* future, we need to look at the long-term picture as a few enlightened people did toward the end of World War II. If you ask the question, Who is the world's superpower today? the answer is easy. The United States. But ask a second question, Who will be the world's *skill* power twenty years from now? The answer is not clear. Whatever answer evolves from that second question is the key to who will be the world's leader in the future.

If the average grant under the old GI Bill were to be escalated by the inflation index, it would now be a grant of more than $11,000, several times more than any student receives today from the federal government. It is true that the GI Bill went only to veterans, but it was given regardless of family income. Today's much smaller Pell Grants go only to those in the lowest income category. In the days of the GI Bill and the years that immediately followed, three-fourths of federal government assistance to students came in the form of grants, one-fourth in loans. Today federal assistance is three-fourths loans, one-fourth grants. Loans often cause a young couple to postpone buying a home or having a family. Worse than that, they distort career choices. Students frequently tell me that they would really like to be teachers or social workers or journalists, but they can make more money to pay off their loans by becoming lawyers or engineers or by working in some other profession—and we end up losing good teachers, social workers, journalists, and people in socially sensitive fields. More significantly for the economy, wages of unskilled workers have been dropping slowly since 1973. Economist Lester Thurow writes, "To return to a world of rising real wages for most Americans, a massive program of reskilling and re-educating the bottom 60 percent of the work force would be needed."[56] We should do it.

In 2001, under the leadership of President George W. Bush, Congress enacted a ten-year tax cut (cash bonus) of $1.35 trillion. What if, instead of that, a decision had been made to use a small portion of that tax cut to shift back to a three-fourths grant, one-fourth loan program, bringing the total available to students—regardless of need—to something approaching what the GI Bill provided? The magazine *Black Issues in Higher Education* had an item on a survey done by the Lumina Foundation for Education, based in Indianapolis; the heading tells the story: "Study: Most Colleges Out of Reach for Low-Income Students."[57] One writer notes: "At four-year public colleges and universities, tuition was equal to 25 percent of the average annual income of a low-income family in 2000. . . . In 1980, the figure was 13 percent."[58] Not surprisingly, student debt has risen rapidly. Do I like a tax cut? Yes. Would the educational program do more for the nation in the long run? By a country mile. Enacting it would require great courage on the part of members of the House and Senate and the administration.

While there is waste in government, as there is in the private sector, adding to the difficulty of using federal revenues for worthy purposes is the widespread belief that there is massive misuse of tax money, which is not generally true, even though candidates of both parties love to tell the electorate how they will cut huge, unnecessary expenditures. The 1978 referendum in California that called for a substantial cut in state and local taxes, known as Proposition 13, passed comfortably. It launched a "tax revolt" that reverberated around the nation. Columnist David Broder observes:

> One poll showed a 38 percent plurality believed that services could continue at the same level, even if revenues were cut by two-fifths, simply by eliminating waste and inefficiency. . . . What in the 1970s had been the nation's model school system . . . fell into disrepair and disrepute. By the time the twentieth anniversary of Proposition 13 came around, California . . . had fallen to forty-second in per-pupil spending on its schools. . . . Although Proposition 13

> was fueled by a revolt of homeowners against rising property taxes, two-thirds of the initial savings went to corporations. . . . In the first year alone, Southern California Edison saved \$54 million; Pacific Gas and Electric, \$90 million; and Pacific Telephone and Telegraph, \$130 million.[59]

Broder also tells of a fascinating fight in Nebraska over a similar tax referendum. Unfortunately, a good education requires a tax burden. A few years ago, I spoke to the Nebraska Press Association on the general topic of building that state's economy. In the counties of Illinois, I had observed that as the average educational level went up, income also rose—as did the taxes collected—with small deviations. I thought I would test this with a state-by-state analysis. As it so happened, Nebraska ranked twenty-fourth in per capita spending on education and precisely twenty-fourth in per capita income. I told them that the lesson to be drawn is clear: Spend more money wisely on education, and you will lift the income level and the economy of Nebraska. That is applicable to the nation also.

If you take the cost of the \$5.5 billion spent on the GI Bill over seven years and add the inflation factor, today it would total approximately \$13 billion per year; add to that the cost of the greater number of students, and it would come to perhaps \$30 billion per year, a sizable amount—but a much smaller percentage of the total budget than the GI Bill was. A solid program could be worked out that would raise the spirit of the nation. Today, there are more young African American males in prison than in college.[60] An improved higher education assistance package by itself will not solve that, but if you combine a good prekindergarten program with adult literacy programs and a greater assist for those wanting to go to college or a trade school, we would dramatically reduce our crime rate and become a more productive and a more humane nation. Over time, that would save money for the taxpayers. The GI Bill repaid the federal government many times—in addition to the other benefits—because those better-educated veterans earned more money and then paid more in taxes.

The most widely read American newspaper columnist for several decades, Walter Lippmann, in 1952 wrote: "We are quite rich enough to defend ourselves, whatever the cost. We must now learn that we are quite rich enough to educate ourselves as we need to be educated."[61] Chinese philosopher Kuan Chung observed: "If you plan for a year, plant a seed. If you plan for ten years, plant a tree. If for a hundred years, teach the people."[62]

Abraham Lincoln's role in the Civil War and in freeing the slaves is so dramatic that some of the less riveting things he did have been ignored. His signing the land-grant college act—after his predecessor James Buchanan had vetoed it—gave higher education a huge boost. At the age of twenty-three, Lincoln ran for the state legislature—and lost—but in his announcement statement, he said, "I view [education] as the most important subject which we as a people can be engaged in."[63] In 2009, the nation will celebrate the two hundredth anniversary of Lincoln's birth. What if instead of simply glowing speeches and bunting and patriotic nothingness, we launched a program that gave significant financial help to everyone who wants to pursue a college education or learn a trade? It would be in the spirit of Lincoln and of the GI Bill and would be a tremendous aid to our grandchildren and generations to come. It would take courage to do it.

Not all social ills can be placed at the feet of education, and on a few issues, the source for our problems is not clear. Robert Putnam notes the decline in civic participation among well-educated people but a greater decline among those with more limited education. As one test of community involvement, participation in clubs, he writes, "Among the burgeoning numbers of college graduates, the average number of club meetings per year fell by 55 percent (from thirteen meetings per year to six), while among high school graduates, the drop in annual meeting attendance was 60 percent (from ten meetings per year to four), and among the dwindling number of Americans who had not completed high school, the drop in annual meeting attendance was 73 percent (from nine meetings per year to two per year)."[64] The entire scene of social interaction shows decline. We are losing a sense of community. Is education responsible? Partially. Is education the remedy? Partially. What has caused that decline, Putnam calls "our central mystery."[65] The massive advent of television into our culture comes at the same time as the decline. That is a partial cause.

As we search for answers to this serious social ill, it is probable that the response in education will require the same quality missing in other areas: Leadership with courage.

Postscript

[Americans] must give to government more constitutional space in which to think, more social distance to facilitate deliberation about the future.

—George Will, *Restoration: Congress Term Limits, and the Recovery of Deliberative Democracy* (1992)

A Few Final Words

SHORTLY BEFORE his death in 1996, NBC commentator John Chancellor wrote: "What the country needs is a peacetime Pearl Harbor to shake it up, to make Americans aware of the trouble they're in. . . . We have weakened ourselves in the way we practice our politics, manage our businesses, teach our children, protect our environment and run our government. . . . They all constitute an interlocking web of lethal trouble for the future."[1]

In order to become stronger, we need leadership that does not pander, that tells us the truth, that gives us a vision of a better tomorrow and the sacrifices we must all make to achieve that vision.

Frank Rich wrote in his *New York Times* column, "We have small ideas, small plans, small schemes."[2] He is correct. It is easy to drift, to make minor adjustments and believe they are grand plans, to do nothing to disturb our comfort, and most Americans are comfortable. With apologies to George Gershwin, we're singing, "Drifting time, and the living is easy." But it is not easy for millions of almost unseen Americans. It is not easy for most people around the world. And it will not be easy for our children and grandchildren if we don't have dreams larger than maintaining the status quo.

Robert Frost once challenged each of us to become a one-person revolution.[3] Less eloquently, I ask the same of you. If you are in a position of responsibility in any one of the four sectors—politics, media, religion, education—be willing to do "that little extra" that ultimately can be meaningful. It may require risking a little, and most of us are risk-averse, but the greatest risk is probably a little embarrassment. But without that small risk, you won't change things.

All of you not in these fields can instill courage in those who are nominal leaders by becoming more involved and by soiling your hands in life's realities yourselves. One simple but significant request: Get together with four of your friends some evening and discuss how you can communicate your concerns to leaders in at least one of these areas, how you can make a difference. Develop a brief agenda for action. It is a small thing, but believe me, it has a real chance of making a difference.

Political scientist and philosopher Hannah Arendt wrote: "Most of the time, in the ordinary course of our lives, we are engaged in behavior. The things we do are predictable and in character. But once in a while, we stop behaving and begin to act."[4] Each of us can act if we learn to care and want to make a difference.

A few years ago, I heard a speaker ask, in the middle of a talk, "Who gave you permission to sit on the sidelines?" We need your involvement; we need your insight; we need your courage; we need your dreams. We don't need you on the sidelines.

Acknowledgments

Notes

Index

Acknowledgments

I AM GRATEFUL to many who played a part in creating this book. The person who translates my typing and scribbling into a word processor so that the publisher can use it is Marilyn Lingle, now a veteran of my manuscripts. Special mention should also go to Pam Gwaltney for her work in my office, and to Katherine McAndrew Keeney, who chased down many footnotes for me. Others who helped through library services or comments on my manuscript or in other ways include John Annable, Chris Barr, Matt Baughman, Frederick Betz, Mazhar Butt, Jody Fagan, Fletcher Farrar, Robert Flannery, Bob Giles, Graham Glover, Robert Gray, Abdul Haqq, John Jackson, Marvin Kalb, Perry Knop, Mike Lawrence, Carol Marin, John Marty, Abner Mikva, Zoe Mikva, Bernard Rapaport, Mark Samuels, David Saperstein, Anthony Scariano, Arthur Simon, Patricia Simon, Sheila Simon, Rick Stetter, Larry Townsend, and James Wall. Elizabeth Brymer, my editor, served valiantly. My wife, Patti, patiently put up with my secluding myself in the study while I pounded out the manuscript. I am sure there are others I should be acknowledging. Like all authors, I do not hold any of them responsible for my views, but I thank them.

Notes

Preface

1. Anthony Lewis, "It Isn't Working," *New York Times*, 1 July 2000.

1. *Pandering in Politics*

1. John Adams, *The Adams Family* (Boston: Little, Brown, 1930), p. 95.
2. James H. Boren quoted in *Peter's Quotations*, ed. Laurence Peter (New York: Morrow, 1997), p. 296.
3. Collins quoted in "Shocking Moments, Great Drama, Big Fears," by Michael Hoyt, *Columbia Journalism Review*, January/February 2001.
4. Robert Putnam, *Bowling Alone* (New York: Simon and Schuster, 2000), pp. 186–87.
5. Walter Shapiro, "Pollster-Bashing Now a Campaign Trend," *USA Today*, 18 August 1999.
6. Quoted in Anthony Lewis, "Who Is Tony Blair?" *New York Times*, 21 April 1997.
7. Elizabeth Drew, *Whatever It Takes: The Real Struggle for Political Power in America* (New York: Viking, 1997), p. 136.
8. Luke 6:26.
9. Plutarch, *The Lives of Noble Grecians and Romans* (Dryden translation), vol. 43 of *Great Books of the Western World* (Chicago: Encyclopedia Britannica, 1952), p. 299.
10. Mario Cuomo, address to College of Trial Lawyers, Boca Raton, Florida, 21 March 1997.
11. Henry Kissinger, *Does America Need a Foreign Policy?* (New York: Simon and Schuster, 2001), p. 288.

12. Brian Mulroney, address, Southern Illinois University Carbondale, 1 November 2001.

13. Kissinger, *Does America Need a Foreign Policy?* p. 252.

14. Ejikeme Obasi, *Nigeria: Starting Over (and Doing It Right)* (Huntington, W.Va.: University Editions, 1998), p. 29.

15. "Foreign Aid Level 'Shameful' Annan Tells Notre Dame Grads," *America*, 3–10 June 2000.

16. Gandhi quoted in Samuel Gupta, "Not a Choice, but a Necessity," *International Herald-Tribune*, 7 October 2002.

17. "Adapting to the New National Security Environment," special report by the U.S. Institute of Peace, Washington, D.C., 1 December 2000.

18. Albright quoted in Andrew J. Bacevich, "A Less Than Splendid Little War," *Woodrow Wilson Quarterly*, winter 2001.

19. Steve Chapman, "Making Friends and Enemies in the Middle East," *Chicago Tribune*, 20 September 2001.

20. William Clinton, "Shaping the Future," *Chicago Tribune*, 13 January 2002.

21. Morrison quoted in Paul Hammel, "Morrison Says Terrorism Feeds Off Inequities," *Omaha World-Herald*, 12 October 2001.

22. *Public Papers of the Presidents of the United States: John F. Kennedy, 1961* (Washington: GPO, 1962), p. 1.

23. Niall Ferguson, "2002," *New York Times Magazine*, 2 December 2001.

24. Leon Aron, "Poor Democracies," *Weekly Standard*, 16 July 2001.

25. Barbara Crossette, "U.N. Chief Faults Reluctance of U.S. to Help in Africa," *New York Times*, 13 May 2000.

26. Moore quoted in Tim Weiner, "More Aid, More Need: Pledges Still Falling Short," *New York Times*, 24 March 2002.

27. Joe Foote, dean of the Walter Cronkite School of Journalism and Telecommunications, Arizona State University, in a letter to Paul Simon, 5 June 2002.

28. Ashcroft quoted in Thomas Eagleton, "The Rule of Law vs. the Rule of Ashcroft," *St. Louis Post-Dispatch*, 2 January 2002.

29. Katharine Seelve, "U.S. Argues War Detainee Shouldn't See a Lawyer," *New York Times*, 1 June 2002.

30. Sensenbrenner quoted in "Judiciary Committee Chairman Says Surveillance Goes Too Far," *Southern Illinoisan*, 2 June 2002.

31. William Safire, "J. Edgar Mueller," *New York Times*, 3 June 2002.

32. Steve Fainaru, "Suspect Held Eight Months Without Seeing a Judge," *Washington Post*, 12 June 2002.

33. Eric Schmitt, "U.S. Will Seek to Fingerprint Visas' Holders," *New York Times*, 5 June 2002.

34. Frank Rich, "Thanks for the Heads-Up," *New York Times*, 25 May 2002.

35. Hutchins quoted in Clifton Fadiman, *Anecdotes* (Boston: Little, Brown, 1985), p. 295.

36. Jacques Barzun, *From Dawn to Decadence* (New York: Harper Collins, 2000), p. 109.

37. Richard Stevenson, "Benefits and Drawbacks to Bush and Gore Proposals for Overhauling Social Security," *New York Times*, 19 May 2000.

38. "Social Security Monsters, Inc." (editorial), *St. Louis Post-Dispatch*, 18 December 2001.

39. Robert W. McChesney, *Rich Media, Poor Democracy* (New York: New Press, 1999), p. xx. Statistics on various countries are from the Justice Department.

40. Kissinger, *Does America Need a Foreign Policy?* p. 35.

41. I am indebted to my colleague Mike Lawrence at the Southern Illinois University Public Policy Institute for compiling these statistics.

42. Charles Wheeler III, "Inmate Population Growth Strains System," *Illinois Tax Facts*, February/March 2000.

43. Data from the Justice Policy Institute, Washington, D.C., quoted in Fox Butterfield, "Study Finds Big Increase in Black Men as Inmates since 1980," *New York Times*, 28 August 2002.

44. Richard A. Mendel, *Less Hype, More Help* (Washington: American Youth Policy Forum, 2000), p. 1.

45. "To Establish Justice, to Insure Domestic Tranquility," report of the Milton Eisenhower Foundation, Washington, D.C,. 1999, p. xvii.

46. Burger quoted in "Education as Crime Prevention," *Research Brief* (newsletter), Center on Crime, Communities and Culture, New York, September 1997.

47. Those desiring more information about this program can receive a free video from the Illinois State Board of Education, 100 North First Street, Springfield, Illinois 62777.

48. "Public Safety," *CURE-NY Newsletter*, winter 2000–2001.

49. J. P. Caulkins, C. P. Rydell, W. Schwabe, and J. Chiesa, "Mandatory Minimum Drug Sentences: Throwing Away the Key or the Taxpayer's Money?" Rand Study MR 827-DPRC, 1997.

50. Katherine Finkelstein, "New York to Offer Addicts Treatment Instead of Prison," *New York Times*, 23 June 2000.

51. Sir George Gipps quoted in Norval Morris, *Maconochie's Gentlemen* (New York: Oxford University Press, 2002), p. xviii.

52. Quoted in Marc Mauer, *Race to Incarcerate* (New York: New Press, 1999), p. 87.

53. FBI and Department of Justice statistics quoted in Mauer, *Race to Incarcerate*, p. 89.

54. Mauer, *Race to Incarcerate*, pp. 87–88.

55. "Study Shows Building Prisons Did Not Prevent Repeat Crimes," *New York Times*, 3 June 2002.

56. Linda Allison-Lewis, *When Someone You Love Has a Gambling Problem* (booklet) (St. Meinrad, Ind.: Abbey Press, 1992).

57. Statement issued by the National Center on Addiction and Substance Abuse, Columbia University, 12 June 2001.

58. "America's Gambling Fever: How Casinos Empty Your Wallet," *U.S. News and World Report*, 14 March 1994.

59. Dr. David Phillips quoted in Sandra Blakeslee, "Suicide Rate Is Higher in 3 Gambling Cities," *New York Times*, 16 December 1997.

60. John Warren Kindt, "U.S. and International Concerns over the Socio-Economic Costs of Legalized Gambling: Greater Than the Illegal Drug Problem?" (statement to the National Gambling Impact Study Commission), 21 May 1998.

61. *Dateline*, NBC, January 1996.

62. Tom Coates, Consumer Credit of Des Moines, in an undated letter to Iowa state legislators.

63. Nader quoted in Tom Batt, "Nader Says Gaming Targets Children," *Las Vegas Review-Journal and Las Vegas Sun*, 13 July 1998.

64. John Egan, "State-Sanctioned Gambling Is a Bad Bet," *U.S. Catholic*, reprint, n.d.

65. Joy quoted in Debra Illingworth Greene, "Gambling Wins and Losses," *Lutheran*, December 1997.

66. Mark Brown, "Bill Black Might Be Mad, but He's Not Crazy," *Chicago Sun-Times*, 6 June 2002.

67. "Washington's Well-Armed Bandits," e-mail bulletin, ouch@ publicampaign, 11 August 1998.

68. Paul Simon, *PS: The Autobiography of Paul Simon* (Chicago: Bonus Books, 1999), p. 306.

69. Hugo Rojas, "Campaign Largess Bought Enron Plenty," *Chicago Sun-Times*, 9 February 2002.

70. Bill Moyers, address to Environmental Grantsmakers Association, Brainerd, Minnesota, 16 October 2001.

71. Jim Hightower, *If the Gods Had Meant Us to Vote They Would Have Given Us Candidates* by (New York: Harper Collins, 2000), p. 270.

72. Ibid., p. 272.

73. Ibid., pp. 267–68.

74. Limbaugh quoted in James Bowman, "The Leader of the Opposition," *National Review*, 6 September 1993.

75. Goldwater quoted by William Moyers, address, San Francisco, 3 December 1997 (available from Public Campaign, Washington, D.C.).

76. Paul Findley, *Silent No More* (Beltsville, Md.: Amana, 2001), p. 243.

77. Moyers quoted in a mailing of the National Health Law Program, Los Angeles, December 2001.

78. William Hartung, "Stop Arming the World," *Bulletin of the Atomic Scientists*, January/February 2001.

79. Elizabeth Olson, "After U.S. Objects, World Fails to Agree to Curb Smoking Ads," *New York Times*, 29 November 2001.

80. Elizabeth Drew, *The Corruption of American Politics* (Woodstock, N.Y.: Overlook Press, 1999), p. 61.

81. Burt Neuborne, "The Supreme Court and Free Speech," *St. Louis University Law Journal*, summer 1998.

82. Johnson quoted in *Reaching for Glory: Lyndon Johnson's Secret White House Tapes, 1964–1965*, ed. Michael Beschloss (New York: Simon and Schuster, 2001), p. 200.

83. Tom Hamburger, Laurie McGinley, and David S. Cloud, "Industries That Back Bush Are Now Seeking Return on Investment," *Wall Street Journal*, 6 March 2001.

84. John Ruggie, "The UN: Bush's Newest Ally?" *Nation*, 31 December 2001.

85. Barbara Crossette, "UN Shivers in a Season of Cost Cuts That Pinch," *New York Times*, 13 March 2002.

86. Henry Bellmon with Pat Bellmon, *The Life and Times of Henry Bellmon* (Tulsa: Council Oaks Books, 1992), p. 305.

87. "Welfare Reform's Darker Side" (editorial), *America*, 19 September 1998.

88. Peter Edelman, "Reforming Welfare—Take Two," *Nation*, 4 February 2002.

89. Thompson quoted in Jason DeParle, "States Struggle to Use Windfall Boon of Shifts in Welfare Law," *New York Times*, 29 August 1999.

90. Patricia White quoted in Michael Janofsky, "West Virginia Pares Welfare, but Poor Remain," *New York Times*, 7 March 1999.

91. "Billboard Tweaks Wellstone," *Minneapolis Star Tribune*, 13 September 1995.

92. Mike Lawrence, Jim Edgar's press secretary, conversation with author.

93. Quoted in James Jeffords, *My Declaration of Independence* (New York: Simon and Schuster, 2001), p. 59.

2. *Pandering in the Media*

1. Keillor quoted in Jim Lehrer, "Why Journalists Rate with Lawyers, Politicians, Pornographers," *International Journalist*, winter 1998–99.

2. Ibid.

3. Douglas quoted in Paul Simon, *The Glass House* (New York: Continuum, 1984), pp. 120–21.

4. Jonathan Alter, "The Media's Balancing Act," *Newsweek*, 8 October 2001.

5. Study by Robert Lichter and Daniel Amundson, Center for Media and Public Affairs, quoted in Steven Stark, "Too Representative Government," *Atlantic Monthly*, May 1995.

6. Marvin Kalb, *One Scandalous Story: Clinton, Lewinsky, and Thirteen Days That Tarnished American Journalism* (New York: Free Press, 2001), p. 273.

7. Ibid., pp. 222–23.

8. Ibid., p. 138.

9. Harold Evans, "Freedom for What?" twentieth annual Frank E. Gannett lecture, Media Studies Center, New York City, 10 December 1997.

10. Tom Rosenstiel, Carl Gottlieb, and Lee Ann Brady, "Time of Peril for TV News," *Columbia Journalism Review,* November/December 2000.

11. Neil Hickey, "Low—and Getting Lower," *Columbia Journalism Review,* September/October 2001.

12. Tim McGuire, president of American Society of Newspaper Editors, annual address, April 2002.

13. Dan Sullivan, professor of media management at the University of Minnesota, quoted in ibid.

14. Ibid.

15. Rowe quoted in Kalb, *One Scandalous Story,* p. 275.

16. Data on news coverage from *Media Monitor,* Center for Media and Public Affairs, Washington, D.C., March/April 1996.

17. Peters quoted in Russ Baker, "The Script," *Columbia Journalism Review,* January/February 2001.

18. Adam Clymer, "Better Campaign Reporting: A View from the Major Leagues," *Political Science,* December 2001.

19. Markle Commission (composed of journalists and academics), quoted in Thomas Johnson, Timothy Boudreau, and Chris Glowaki, "Turning the Spotlight Inward: How Five Leading News Organizations Covered the Media in the 1992 Presidential Election," *Journalism and Mass Communication Quarterly,* autumn 1996.

20. Albert R. Hunt, "Don't Stop at McCain-Feingold," *Wall Street Journal,* 21 February 2002.

21. Paul Taylor, "Holding an Election on the Cheap," *Political Standard,* July 2001.

22. Walter Cronkite, preface to *The Case for Free Air Time,* by Paul Taylor (Washington, D.C.: Alliance for Better Campaigns, 2002).

23. Cronkite quoted in *Writer's Digest,* September 2001, p. 4.

24. "Gouging Democracy" (booklet), Alliance for Better Campaigns, Washington, D.C., 2001, p. 3.

25. Putnam, *Bowling Alone,* p. 218.

26. Frederick Betz, note to author, 3 June 2002.

27. Bush quoted in Christopher Hanson, "God and Man on the Campaign Trail," *Columbia Journalism Review,* November/December 2000.

28. J. Bottum and William Kristol, "Faith Talk," *Weekly Standard,* 11 September 2000.

29. Patricia Williams, "Infallible Justice," *Nation,* 7 October 2002.

30. James Wall, *Hidden Treasures: Searching for God in Modern Culture* (Chicago: Christian Century Press, 1997), p. 23.

31. Bruce Jones, *Peacemaking in Rwanda* (London: Lynne Rienner, 2001), p. 105.

32. Ibid.

33. Leonard Downie Jr. and Robert Kaiser, *The News about the News* (New York: Alfred Knopf, 2002), pp. 7 and 247.

34. Ibid., pp. 151–52.

35. John Maxwell Hamilton and George A. Krimsky, "'Juju' News from Abroad," *Gannett Center Journal*, fall 1989.

36. Seaton quoted in Michael Parks, "Foreign News: What's Next?" *Columbia Journalism Review*, January/February 2002. *f*

37. Laidi quoted in Serge Schmemann, "Where McDonald's Sits Down with Arab Nationalists," *New York Times*, 2 February 2002.

38. Kissinger, *Does America Need a Foreign Policy?* p. 27.

39. Seymour Topping, *Bringing the World Home* (Roslyn, Va.: Freedom Forum, 1999), p. 11.

40. Garrick Utley, "The Shrinking of Foreign News," *Foreign Affairs*, March/April 1997.

41. Parks, "Foreign News."

42. Kalb quoted in Bill Kirtz, "Downhill Slide?" *Quill*, January/February 1999.

43. For more details on the author's efforts in this area, see Simon, *PS*, pp. 297–302.

44. Bill Carter, "Fox TV Pulls 'The Chamber,' a Reality Show," *New York Times*, 29 January 2002.

45. Martin Simon quoted in *Life: Classic Faces* (New York: Macmillan, 1991), pp. 86–87.

46. Executive summary, *National Television Violence Study* (Studio City, Calif.: Mediascope, 1995), p. vi.

47. Ibid., p. 24.

48. Study by Leonard Eron et al., quoted in Dave Grossman and Gloria DeGaetano, *Stop Teaching Our Kids to Kill* (New York: Crown, 1999), p. 133.

49. Minow quoted in ibid., p. 134.

50. *Preventing Violence in America* (National Commission for the Prevention of Youth Violence, 2000), p. 25.

51. N. Pecora, J. P. Murray, and E. Wartella, *Children and Television: 50 Years of Research* (Hillsdale, N.J.: Lawrence Erlbaum, 2002).

52. Plato quoted in William Bennett, ed., *The Book of Virtues* (New York: Simon and Schuster, 1993), p. 17.

53. "Violence," *Dialogue*, winter 1993.

54. Carey Goldberg, "Family Killings Jolt a Tranquil Town," *New York Times*, 3 February 1997.

55. Crouch quoted in Andrea Sachs and Susanne Washburn, "A Company under Fire," *Time*, 12 June 1995.

56. Bennett quoted in ibid.

57. Robert Lichter, Linda Lichter, and Dan Amundson, *Merchandising Mayhem* (Washington, D.C.: Center for Media and Public Affairs, 1999), p. 1.

58. Gina Kolata, "Study Finds More Links Between TV and Violence," *New York Times*, 29 March 2002. Copyright 2002 by The New York Times Co. Reprinted by permission.

59. William Safire, *New York Times*, 4 May 2000, quoted in McChesney, *Rich Media, Poor Democracy*, p. xxviii.

60. Zachariah Chafee Jr., "The Press under Pressure," *Nieman Reports*, April 1948.

61. Downie and Kaiser, *The News about the News*, p. 96.

62. Roberts quoted in ibid., p. 97.

63. *Congressional Record*, 15 June 1995.

64. "CBS Radio to Get Five More Stations in St. Louis Market," *St. Louis Post-Dispatch*, 20 September 1997.

65. Jeffrey Chester and Gary Larson, "Whose First Amendment?" *American Prospect*, 17 December 2001.

66. Press release, Federal Communication Commission, 12 March 2001.

67. Daniel J. Rapella, "The Analysis of the Effects of Consolidation on the Radio Industry," unpublished study prepared for Gannon University, fall 1999.

68. Letter to author, 9 August 1996. Because the letter writer still has substantial financial interests in radio, he did not want his name used.

69. Quoted in Downie and Kaiser, *The News about the News*, p. 83. In the interest of full disclosure, it should be noted that the author of this book owns some Knight Ridder stock.

70. Jones quoted in "The Buck Stops Here," *Media Studies Journal*, spring/summer 1996.

71. Data from unpublished research by Cindy J. Price, who teaches in the communications field at the University of Wyoming.

72. Leo Bogart, "What Does It All Mean?" *Media Studies Journal*, spring/summer 1996.

73. Neil Hickey, "Tribune Beams Toward a Multimedia Future," *Columbia Journalism Review*, May/June 2000.

74. Marion Just, "The Budget Game," *Columbia Journalism Review*, November/December 1999.

75. Rosenstiel, Gottlieb, and Brady, "Time of Peril for TV News."

76. Wyden quoted in Neil Hickey, "Unshackling Big Media," *Columbia Journalism Review*, July/August 2001.

77. Turner quoted in "All Together Now," *Electronic Media*, 15 December 1997, quoted in McChesney, *Rich Media, Poor Democracy*, p. 18.

78. McChesney, *Rich Media, Poor Democracy*, p. xxii.

3. *Pandering in Religion*

1. Will Durant, *The Reformation* (New York: Simon and Schuster, 1957), p. 514.

2. James Fallows, "The Invisible Poor," *New York Times Magazine*, 19 March 2000.

3. Niebuhr quoted in Wall, *Hidden Treasures*, p. 103.

4. Kenneth Woodward, "God and Mammon," *Newsweek*, 21 February 2001.

5. Quoted in Rachel Mikva, *Broken Tablets* (Woodstock, Vt.: Jewish Lights, 1999), p. 38.

6. Jean Behtke Elshtain quoted in *Religion, Politics and the American Experience*, ed. Edith Blumhofer (Tuscaloosa: University of Alabama Press, 2002), pp. 19–20.

7. David Beckman and Arthur Simon, *Grace at the Table* (New York: Paulist Press, 1990), p. 196.

8. Marty quoted in "Spiritual America," *U.S. News and World Report*, 4 April 1994.

9. Eileen Lindner of the National Council of Churches, quoted in Lisa Bertagnoli, "Olympic Torch Casts Light on Mormon Faith," *Chicago Tribune*, 24 February 2002.

10. Robert Wuthnow, "Mobilizing Civic Engagement," quoted in Putnam, *Bowling Alone*, p. 78.

11. Bennett quoted in James Carroll, "The Virtue Bennett Missed," *Boston Globe*, 23 May 1995.

12. Marilyn Jones, "Seminary President Envisions Expanded Role for Church," *Christian Science Sentinel*, 4 March 2002.

13. General letter of appeal, 13 May 2002.

14. Editorial, *Business Week*, 27 September 1999, p. 92.

15. Robert Fogel, interview by Frederic Smoler, *American Heritage*, July/August 2001.

16. Paul Wilkes, *Excellent Protestant Congregations* (Louisville: Westminster John Knox, 2001), pp. 168–69.

17. Adolf Hitler, *Mein Kampf* (New York: Hurst and Blackett, 1942), p. 46.

18. *Official Report of the Fifth Baptist World Congress*, quoted in William Allen, "How Baptists Assessed Hitler," *Christian Century*, 1–8 September 1982.

19. Dr. John R. Sampey, quoted in Allen, "How Baptists Assessed Hitler."

20. Dr. Charles Leek, *Alabama Baptist*, 6 September 1934, quoted in Allen, "How Baptists Assessed Hitler."

21. Tom McGrath, "Editor's Note," *U.S. Catholic*, July 1998.

22. Barbara Ehrenreich, review of *Down and Out, On the Road*, by Kenneth Kusmer, *New York Times Book Review*, 20 January 2002.

23. "The Uses of American Power" (editorial), *New York Times*, 3 March 2002.

24. Lynda C. Carter, in behalf of President Jerry Kieschnick, e-mail to all Lutheran Church–Missouri Synod clergy, 18 April 2002.

25. Hackett quoted in "Lead the Fight: World Hunger" (editorial), *St. Louis Post-Dispatch*, 26 May 2001.

26. Quoted in editorial, *Scranton Times*, 7 February 2001.

27. "Fire Kills 3 Kids, 4 Adults in Poverty-Stricken Family," *Chicago Tribune*, 25 January 2002.

28. "Poverty Affects Breast Cancer," *St. Louis Post-Dispatch*, 3 April 2002.

29. Amos 5:21–24 and 2:6–7.

30. John Annable, note to author, 3 June 2002.

31. Mikva, *Broken Tablets*, p. xx.

32. Hartford Seminary Institute on Religion Research, quoted in *Just Watching*, bulletin of Wheatridge Ministries, Itasca, Illinois.

33. Qur'an 2:177.

34. Vines quoted in Susan Sachs, "Baptist Pastor Attacks Islam, Inciting Cries of Intolerance," *New York Times*, 15 June 2002.

35. Abba Eban, "Judaism, Christianity, Islam," lecture at St. Thomas College, 1987.

36. Abdul Haqq, letter to author, 17 June 2002.

37. *Lutheran*, February 2002.

38. Hubbard quoted in H. L. Mencken, ed., *A New Dictionary of Quotations on Historical Principles* (New York: Knopf, 1966), p. 1,020.

39. Sarah Meyre, "Putting Religion to the Test," *Jerusalem Report*, 9 September 2002.

40. Quoted in statement by Senator Dennis DeConcini, *Congressional Record* (8 October 1991), S 14609.

41. David Saperstein, conversation with author, 6 June 2002.

42. Quoted in Wall, *Hidden Treasures*, p. 84.

43. *The Arab Human Development Report 2002* (New York: United Nations Development Programme, 2002).

44. Sen quoted in Richard Bernstein, "How Freedom Pays Off in Economic Well-Being," *New York Times*, 20 September 1999.

45. Graham Fuller, "The Future of Political Islam," *Foreign Affairs*, March/April 2002.

46. Andrea Stone, "In Poll, Islamic World Says Arabs Not Involved in 9/11," *USA Today*, 27 February 2002.

47. Baig quoted in Laurie Goodstein, "O Ye of Much Faith!" *New York Times*, 2 June 2002.

48. Pascal, *Pensees*, bk. 14, quoted in *Dictionary of Political Quotations*, ed. Lewis Eigen and Jonathon Siegel (New York: Macmillan, 1993), p. 614.

49. Sharon Waxman, "Radical, Retaliatory and Right There on British Bookshelves," *Washington Post*, 3 March 2002.

50. Khalid Duran, *Children of Abraham* (Hoboken, N.J.: Ktav, 2001), pp. 17–18.

51. Ibid., p. 19.

52. Hugh Goddard, *Christians and Muslims: From Double Standards to Mutual Understanding* (Richmond, Eng.: Curzon, 1995).

53. Maximus the Confessor, quoted in John Lamoreaux, "Early East-

ern Christian Responses to Islam," *Medieval Christian Perceptions of Islam: A Book of Essays,* ed. John Tolan (New York: Garland, 1996), p. 14.

54. Rollin Armour Sr., *Islam, Christianity and the West* (Maryknoll, N.Y.: Orbis, 2002), pp. 71–73.

55. *The Adams-Jefferson Letters,* ed. Lester J. Cappon (Chapel Hill: University of North Carolina Press, 1959), pp. 333–35.

56. Martin Marty, *Politics, Religion and the Common Good* (San Francisco: Jossey-Bass, 2000), pp. 23–24.

57. Rogers quoted in *Daily Telegrams,* vol. 2 of *Will Rogers Says,* ed. Reba Collins (Oklahoma City: Will Rogers Memorial and Research Center, 1993), p. 32.

58. Putnam, *Bowling Alone,* p. 409.

59. Ram Cnaan, "Our Hidden Safety Net," *Brookings Review,* spring 1999.

60. Micah 6:8.

61. Martin Luther King, *Strength to Love* (New York: Harper and Row, 1963), p. 37.

4. *Pandering in Education*

1. *Report of the National Education Commission on Time and Learning,* rev. ed. (Peterborough, N.H., 2000), pp. 11–12.

2. *Report of the National Education Commission on Time and Learning* (Peterborough, N.H., 1994), p. 13.

3. William T. Harris quoted in ibid., p. 21.

4. Linda Remington quoted in ibid., p. 23.

5. Thelma Farley, conversation with author, 4 June 2002.

6. James G. Ward, *Teacher Quality* (Urbana: University of Illinois, Institute of Government and Public Affairs, n.d.), p. 11.

7. Carolyn Shields and Steven Oberg, *From Inquiry to Practice: Year-Round Schooling* (Bloomington, Ind.: Phi Delta Kappa, 2000), p. 5.

8. Richard Alcorn, unpublished study (available from the National Association for Year-Round Education, P.O. Box 711386, San Diego, CA 92171).

9. Harris Cooper, Barbara Nye, Kelly Charlton, James Lindsay, and Scott Greathouse, "The Effects of Summer Vacation on Achievement Test Scores," *Review of Educational Research,* fall 1996.

10. Joseph F. Haenn quoted in Carolyn Kneese, *Year-Round Learning* (San Diego: National Association for Year-Round Education, 2000), p. 24.

11. Karl Alexander and Doris Entwisle, "Summer Slide in the City: A Case for Year-Round Schooling?" Department of Sociology, Johns Hopkins University, 26 June 1998, quoted in Gerald Bracey, "What They Did on Vacation," *Washington Post*, 16 January 2002.

12. "Back to Reading," *USA Today*, 13 September 2000, p. 1D.

13. *Report of the National Education Commission*, p. 26.

14. "Milwaukee School Results Noted by White House Domestic Policy Council," *Year-Rounder* (bulletin of the National Association for Year-Round Education, San Diego), winter 2001.

15. Jill Parker, "The Idea Doesn't Fly," *USA Today*, 25 June 1996.

16. Marilyn Stenvall, "Is Summer School the Answer or the Problem?" *Education Week*, 23 May 2001.

17. "Texas Bucks the Trend," *Year-Rounder*, fall 2001.

18. Quoted in *Report of the National Education Commission*, p. 15.

19. Kissinger, *Does America Need a Foreign Policy?* p. 10.

20. Lloyd Elliott, "Restructuring American Education," *Education Week*, 13 February 2002. Reprinted with permission from the author.

21. Oliver Wendell Holmes, *The Autocrat of the Breakfast Table*, quoted in Mencken, *New Dictionary of Quotations*, p. 332.

22. Linda Jacobson, "Looking to France," *Education Week*, 11 July 2001.

23. Barbara Kantrowitz and Pat Wingert, "The Right Way to Read," *Newsweek*, 29 April 2002.

24. Isabell Sawhill, "Kids Need an Early Start," *Blueprint*, fall 1999.

25. The author is grateful to John Homan, Karen Binder, Tracy James, Deb Sauerhage, Christi Mathis, and John Sharp of the *Carbondale Southern Illinoisan* for articles on test scores and spending beginning 18 November 2001.

26. For information about the Earhart school, see the excellent article by Ray Quintanilla, "Small Wonder," *Chicago Tribune Magazine*, 7 April 2002.

27. Elizabeth Olson, "U.S. Gets Too Few U.N. Jobs, Report Says," *New York Times*, 5 August 2001.

28. Thomas Friedman, "Run, Osama, Run," *New York Times*, 23 January 2002.

29. Geoff Porter, "Lost in Translation at the FBI," *New York Times*, 1 June 2002. Copyright 2002 *New York Times*.

30. Elana Shohamy and Smadar Donitsa-Schmidt, *Jews vs. Arabs: Language Attitudes and Stereotypes* (Tel Aviv University, 1988), p. 46.

31. Elana Shohamy, e-mail to author, 11 June 2002.

32. Quotation and other information about doctorate degrees cited in Linton Weeks, "You're the Dr.," *Washington Post*, 18 March 2002.

33. James quoted in ibid.

34. Michael Sovern, former president of Columbia University, conversation with author, March 20, 2003.

35. William Fulbright, interview, *New York Times*, 26 June 1986.

36. Kissinger, *Does America Need a Foreign Policy?* p. 286.

37. Putnam, *Bowling Alone*, p. 35.

38. David Koehler, "Convergence and Restricted Preference Maximizing under Simple Majority Rule: Results from a Computer Simulation of Committee Choice in Two-Dimensional Space," *American Political Science Review*, March 2001.

39. Allan Nevins, "What's the Matter with History?" *Saturday Review of Literature*, 4 February 1939.

40. Alan Sokal, "Transgressing the Boundaries: Toward a Transformative Hermeneutics of Quantum Gravity," *Social Text*, spring/summer 1996.

41. Quoted in Keith Olson, *The GI Bill, the Veterans, and the Colleges* (Lexington: University Press of Kentucky, 1974), pp. 21–22.

42. Quoted in *The New Veteran* (New York: Reynal and Hitchcock, 1945), pp. 123–24, quoted in *American Quarterly*, December 1973.

43. James B. Conant, "Annual Report of the President of the University," *Harvard Alumni Bulletin*, 3 February 1945; 22 January 1944.

44. A. J. Brumbaugh, "Planning Education for Returning Members of the Armed Forces," *23rd Yearbook, American Association of Teachers Colleges*, quoted in Keith Olson, *G.I. Bill*.

45. Willard W. Aller, "Which Veterans Should Go to College?" *Ladies Home Journal*, May 1945, quoted in Keith Olson, *G.I. Bill*.

46. Robert Hutchins, "The Threat to American Education," *Collier's*, 30 December 1944.

47. Tyrus Hillway, "GI Joe and the Colleges," *Journal of Higher Education*, June 1945.

48. Rankin quoted in *Preparing for Ulysses: Politics and Veterans During World War II* (New York: Columbia University Press, 1969), p. 108.

49. Edwin Kiester Jr., "The GI Bill May Be the Best Deal Ever Made by Uncle Sam," *Smithsonian*, November 1994.

50. Colomery quoted in House Committee on World War Veterans' Legislation, *Hearings on H.R. 3817 and S. 1767* (Washington: GPO, 1944), p. 396.

51. Fish quoted in *New York Times*, 6 April 1942, quoted in Keith Olson, *G.I. Bill*.

52. Kiester, "The GI Bill."

53. Conant quoted in Charles Murphy, "GI's at Harvard," *Life*, 17 June 1946, quoted in Keith Olson, *G.I. Bill*.

54. "GI Grinds," *Newsweek*, 1 April 1946.

55. William Brock, address to the National Academy of Human Resources, New York, 2 November 2000.

56. Lester Thurow, "Falling Wages, Failing Policy," *Dollars and Sense*, September/October 1996.

57. "Study: Most Colleges Out of Reach for Low-Income Students," *Black Issues in Higher Education*, 31 January 2002.

58. Robert Shireman, "Enrolling Economic Diversity," *New York Times*, 4 May 2002.

59. David Broder, *Democracy Derailed* (New York: James Silberman, 2000), pp. 46–47.

60. Deborah Prothrow-Stith, *Deadly Consequences* (New York: Harper Perennial, 1991), p. 163.

61. Walter Lippmann, "Citizens and Their Schools," quoted in *Book of 20th Century American Quotations*, ed. Stephen Donadio et al. (New York: Warner Books, 1992), p. 162.

62. Kuan Chung, *Book of Master Kuan*, vol. 1 (1970), p. 12, quoted in *Respectfully Quoted*, ed. Suzy Platt (Washington: Library of Congress, 1989), p. 98.

63. *Collected Works of Abraham Lincoln*, ed. Roy Basler et al., vol. 1 (New Brunswick, N.J.: Rutgers University Press), p. 8.

64. Putnam, *Bowling Alone*, p. 62.

65. Ibid., p. 187.

Postscript

1. John Chancellor, *Peril and Promise: A Commentary on America* (New York: Harper and Row, 1991), p. 23.

2. Frank Rich (columnist), *New York Times,* 1 June 1997.

3. "Build Soil": A Political Pastoral, *The Poetry of Robert Frost,* ed. Edward Lathem (New York: Henry Holt, 1979), p. 324.

4. Arendt quoted in paper by Bernard Rapaport, Waco, Texas, n.d.

Index

ABC, 11, 49, 59, 73, 80, 83
Abscam, 17
ACT scores, 142
Adams, John, 4, 134
Afghanistan, 16, 19
Africa, 14, 18, 76, 77, 104, 110, 129. *See also names of specific countries*
African Americans, 28, 40, 126–27, 155, 172
Air Force, U.S., 44, 167
Albright, Madeleine, 14
Algeria, 9
Allah, 73, 100, 117
Alliance for Better Campaigns, 70
Alter, Jonathan, 63
American Academy of Pediatrics, 82
American Bar Association, 50
American Civil Liberties Union, 82
American Enterprise Institute, 16
American Federation of Teachers, 149
American Federation of Television and Radio Artists, 85
American Legion, 53, 165, 167–68
American Medical Association, 88
American Political Science Association, 69, 164
American Political Science Review, 163–64
American Psychological Association, 88
American Society of Newspaper Editors, 66–67, 78, 79, 81
American Veterans Committee, 166
Amos (prophet), 110, 116, 117
Annable, John, 116
Annan, Kofi, 13, 17
Antipater, King, 7
Arab Human Development Report 2002, The, 127
Arabic, 129, 156–58
Arabs, 119, 127–28, 131, 157–58
Arendt, Hannah, 177
Arizona, 49, 119
Arlington National Cemetery, 84
Armour, Rollin, 133
Aron, Leon, 16
Arthur Andersen, 42
Ashcroft, John, 18, 20, 42
Associated Press, 19, 61, 79, 115–16
Attorney General, U.S., 18, 20

Baig, Naeem, 131
Baker, Howard, 53
Baltimore, Maryland, 143
Baltimore Sun, 159
Bangkok, Thailand, 162
Baptists, 109–11, 118, 122
Bardstown, Kentucky, 142
BBC, 80
Beacon schools, 140–41
Belfast, 100
Belgium, 150
Bellmon, Henry, 52–54
Bennett, William, 87, 105
Berlin Wall, 60
Betz, Frederick, 72
Bible, 7, 103, 110, 114, 117, 135
bin Laden, Osama, 11, 156
Black Issues in Higher Education, 171
Bloomberg, Michael, 41
Bosnia, 83, 130
Boston, 110

Index

Boston University, 105
Bowling Alone (Putnam), 5, 72, 135, 162, 163
Brandeis University, 164
Bread for the World, 104, 106, 115, 123
Brethren, 106
Briggs, Mike, 65
Bringing the World Home (booklet), 81
Britain, 24, 34, 36, 76, 150. *See also* England
Brock, William, 169–70
Broder, David, 171–72
Brookings Institution, 151
Brown, Mark, 40
Buchanan, James, 173
Buddhists and Buddhism, 111, 119, 128
Buehrens, John, 112
Buffett, Warren, 37
Bulletin of the Atomic Scientists, 48
Burger, Warren, 29
Bush, George H. W., 9, 10, 24, 74, 83, 122
Bush, George W., xi, 23, 90, 97, 113, 129, 151, 152, 170; administration of, 42, 48, 55, 56, 156; campaign of, 4, 50
Business Week (magazine), 108
Butt, Mazhar, 130

Cairo (Ill.) High School, 153
Califano, Joseph, 37
California, 28, 44; and education, 140–41, 142–43, 145–46, 171–72; University of, 37, 84, 89, 91
Canada and Canadians, 27, 35, 76, 114
Carbondale (Ill.) Community High School, 153
Carter, Jimmy, 16, 24, 70, 122, 126, 127
Castro, Fidel, 154
Catholics, Roman, 105, 110, 118, 131; and Catholic Relief Services, 106, 115; in Europe, 100, 101, 109, 129; and politics, 53, 74; and public policy, 38, 56, 122
CBS, 59, 61, 80, 83, 92–93, 96, 97
Center for Defense Information, 113
Center for International Research, 79
Center for Media and Public Affairs, 88
Chad, 15
Chafee, Zacariah, Jr., 91
Chancellor, John, 176
Chapman, Steve, 14
Charles V, 100
Chicago, 83, 96, 108, 132, 149, 154; University of, 20–21, 108, 122, 159, 166
Chicago Sun-Times, 40, 42, 65
Chicago Tribune, 14, 64, 78, 95
Children's Defense Fund, 55
Childs, Marquis, 166
Chile, 9
China, 113, 173
Chiquita, 45–46
Christian Coalition, 121
Christian Democrats, 122
Christians and Christianity, 44, 100–105, 109–12, 114–19, 121–23, 128–29; and the Crusades, 129, 132–33; in the United States, 73–74, 105, 134. *See also names of specific denominations*
Christians and Muslims: From Double Standards to Mutual Understanding, 132
Christian Science Monitor, 85
Christopher, Warren, 11
Chung, Kuan, 173
Church of England, 100–101
Church of Jesus Christ of Latter-day Saints, 104
Church of the Holy Sepulcher, 133
CIA, 61, 156
Cincinnati, 93
Civil War, 83, 111, 173
Clinton, Bill, 6, 61, 122; administration of, 42, 49; and education, 14–15; and international relations, 11, 100; and social security, 22, 23; and taxes, 24–25; and welfare, 54, 55
Clymer, Adam, 69
CNN, 59, 80, 98
Coats, Dan, 40
Cold War, 14, 16
Collins, Gail, 4
Colomery, Harry, 167–68
Colorado, 110
Columbia Journalism Review, 66, 79
Columbia University, 37, 89, 95–96, 160, 169
Columbine High School, 110
Commissioner of Education, U.S., 140
Communism, 2, 20–21, 53
Conant, James B., 166, 169
Condit, Gary, 61

Index

Congress, U.S., 3, 10, 49–51, 56, 126, 170; and campaign contributions, 41–42, 45, 49–50; and education, 166, 169; and the media, 63, 94; and the poor, 54, 113, 114. *See also* House of Representatives, U.S.; Republicans, in Congress; Senate, U.S.
Congress Extended Year-Round School, 144–45
Connecticut, 117
Constitution, U.S., 20, 48, 133; First Amendment to, 90, 135
Consumer Credit, 38
Cook County jail, 31
Costa Rica, 9
Court of Appeals, 114
Cox, Tony, 83
Cronkite, Walter, 70, 71, 72, 94
Crouch, Stanley, 87
Crusades, 129, 132–33
C-SPAN, 72, 98
Cuba, 4, 154, 155
Cuban Americans, 4
Cuomo, Mario, 7–8
Cyprus, 52

Dallaire, Romeo, 76
Dallas, Texas, 118, 146, 151
Dana College, 168
Danforth, John, 23
Defense Department, U.S., 20, 44
Deists, 134
Democratic Party, 42, 46, 69
Democrats, 22, 23, 26, 43, 45, 122; in Congress, 52, 57
Denmark, 12, 113
Dinkins, David, 93
Directors Guild, 85
Disabled American Veterans, 166
Dodd, Chris, 93, 162
Dole, Bob, 68
Douglas, Paul, 62
Dow Jones, 22
Downie, Leonard, Jr., 77, 92
Doyle, Dennis, 139
Drew, Elizabeth, 7, 48–49
Durham, North Carolina, 143

Earhart Elementary School, Chicago, 154
Eban, Abba, 118
Economist (periodical), 80
Ecuador, 78
Edgar, Jim, 57–58
Education, U.S. Commissioner of, 140
Edwards, Edwin, 38
Egan, John, 38
Egypt, 12
Ehrenreich, Barbara, 112
Einstein, Albert, 21
Eisenhower, Milton, 28
Elliott, Lloyd H., 147–48
England, 35, 67, 80, 100–101, 111, 168; London, 6, 9, 131. *See also* Britain
English, 120, 132, 159
Enron Corporation, 42, 49
Episcopal Church of the Apostles, 107
Episcopalians, 74, 122
Eron, Dr. Leonard, 89
Ethiopia, 16, 132
Europe, 27, 100, 131; eastern, 9, 64; western, 2, 24, 45, 114, 121–22, 161. *See also names of specific countries*
European Union, 17
Evans, Harold, 64
Excellent Protestant Congregations, 109

Fallows, James, 101
Farley, Thelma, 140–41
FBI, 17, 19, 156–57
Federal Communications Commission (FCC), 93, 97
Federal Express, 43
Feingold, Russ, 43, 49, 93
Findley, Paul, 47
Fish, Hamilton, 168
Florida, 4, 78, 167
Fogel, Robert, 108–9
Foote, Joe, 137
Ford, Gerald, 70
Ford's Theatre, 46
Foreign Affairs (periodical), 80
Fox Television, 80, 83
France, 79, 100, 113, 131, 132–33; education in, 140, 149–51
Freedom Forum, 64, 79, 81
Freedom House, 127
French, 160

Index

Friedman, Thomas, 156
Friends (Quakers), 106, 111
Frost, Robert, 176
Fulbright, William, 162
Fulbright program, 78, 161, 162
Fuller, Graham, 130

Gallup polls, 3, 130
Gandhi, Mahatma, 13, 112
GED, 55
General Electric, 97
Georgia, 167
German, 159
Germany, 3, 40, 109–10, 123; education in, 139, 140, 159
Gershwin, George, 176
Ghana, 27
GI Bill, 165–71, 172
Gibson, John, 167
Gilboa, Israel, 119
God, 58, 116, 121, 132; in the Bible, 119, 135; and the United States, 74, 103, 110
Goldwater, Barry, 47
Gonzalez, Elian, 4
Gore, Al, 4, 74, 90
Graham, Billy, 129
Gray, Robert, 106
Greece, 150
Greenlaw, William, 107
Grinnell College, 162
Gulf War, 122
Gurdjieff, George, 99

Habitat for Humanity, 104, 124
Hackett, Kenneth, 115
Hamilton, Alexander, 4, 40, 43
Handgun Control Inc., 97
Haqq, Abdul, 118
Harris, Irving, 149
Hartford Courant, 65
Hartford Seminary, 117
Hartigan, Neil, 57
Harvard, 39, 91, 128, 159, 169
Hastert, Dennis, 22
Head Start, 151
Health and Human Resources Department, U.S., 56
Hearst-Argyle Television, 71
Hebrew, 157
Hernandez, Angel, 156
Hindus, 75, 111, 128, 129, 132
Hispanic people, 28, 156
History Channel, 98
Hitler, Adolf, 100, 109, 123
Holloway, Alfretta, 155
Holmes, Oliver Wendell, 149
Holocaust, 121
Holy Land, 133
Honduras, 106
Hoover, Herbert, 74
House of Representatives, U.S., 6, 25, 53, 58, 115; and campaign contributions, 43, 44; committees of, 42, 156, 166; and education, 162, 167, 171; and foreign aid, 16, 17, 124; Republicans in, 19, 22, 47
Hubbard, Elbert, 119
Humphrey, Hubert, 6, 90
Hunt, Al, 70
Hutchins, Robert, 21, 166
Hyde, Henry, 156

Idaho, University of, 162
Illinois, 39, 46, 50, 57, 62, 110; Carbondale, 106, 153; education in, 139, 153, 172; prisons in, 27, 30–31; University of, 27, 37, 98, 126. *See also* Chicago; Southern Illinois University
Independent Sector, 124
India, 9, 10, 42, 74–75, 128, 129, 130, 132
Indiana, 37
Indianapolis, 171
Indonesia, 131
Infinity Corporation, 92
Institute for Mental Health Initiatives, 86
International Herald Tribune, 11
Internet, 5, 38, 98
Iowa, 34, 38, 162
Iran, 73
Iraq, 64, 113, 152
Ireland, 75, 100
Isaiah (prophet), 117
Islam, 118, 130, 132. *See also* Muslims
Israel, 12, 15, 61, 118, 119, 157–58
Israelis, 100, 131
Italy, 3, 77, 150

Jacksonville, Florida, 167
Jacor Communications, 93

James, William, 159–60
Japan, 2, 3, 9, 24, 84, 162; education in, 139, 140; and the poor, 113, 114
Japanese Americans, 18
Jefferson, Thomas, 40, 74, 134
Jeffords, James, 76, 137
Jehovah's Witnesses, 134
Jerusalem, 133
Jesus, 7, 74, 103, 116, 117, 134, 159
Jews, 103, 106, 119, 128; discrimination against, 126, 129; and education, 157–58; in the United States, 105, 110–11, 112; violence against, 100, 133. *See also* Israel; Judaism
Johns Hopkins University, 143
Johnson, Dr. Jeffrey G., 89
Johnson, Lyndon, 49–50, 162
Jones, Alex, 94
Jordan, 115
Joy, JoDean, 39
Judaism, 73. *See also* Jews
Justice Department, U.S., 19–20, 36, 92

Kalamazoo College, 162
Kalb, Marvin, 60, 64, 81
Kansas, 78; State University, 78, 85
Keillor, Garrison, 60
Keim, Roland, 110
Kelly, Richard, 17
Kennedy, John F., 15, 74, 90
Kennedy, Ted, 43
Kennedy Center, 49
Kentucky, 66, 110, 142
Kilpatrick, James J., 77
Kindt, John Warren, 37
King, Martin Luther, 111, 135–36
Kissinger, Henry, 9, 10, 27, 79, 147, 163
Knight Ridder, 94
Koppel, Ted, 64
Korematsu, 18
Kosovo, 11
Kunkle, Dr. Dale, 89
Kuwait, 131

Lack, Andrew, 77
Laidi, Zaki, 79
Lamb, Brian, 72
LaSalle County, Illinois, 82
Latin, 159
Latin America, 9, 127–28, 162. *See also names of specific countries*
Leal, Maria, 108
Lehrer, Jim, 60, 72
Levy, Chandra, 61
Lewinsky, Monica, 6, 49, 61, 75
Lewis, Anthony, ix
Lexington (Kentucky) Herald-Leader, 66
Liberia, 16–17
Lieberman, Joseph, x
Life (magazine), 84
Limbaugh, Rush, 47
Lincoln, Abraham, 15, 122, 173
Lindner, Carl, 45–46
Linowitz, Sol, 53
Lippmann, Walter, 173
London, England, 131
Lorraine, France, 133
Los Angeles Times, 64, 73, 77, 78, 80, 95
Louisiana, 160
Loza, Julio, 108
Lumina Foundation for Education, 171
Luther, Martin, 129
Lutherans, 100, 101, 102, 105–6, 109, 117–18, 122; Missouri Synod of, 106, 108, 114
Luxembourg, 150
Lynwood, Washington, 118

Maconochie, Captain, 34
Madjid, Nurcholish, 131
Maine, 49, 134
Malachi (Bible), 119
Malawi, 110
Mali, 27
Manhattan (Kansas) Mercury, 78
Marin, Carol, 96
Marion Medical Mission, 110
Marshall, George, 2–3
Marshall Plan, 2–3, 11, 165
Marty, Martin, 104, 134
Maryland, 139, 143–44; University of, 115
Matthew, Gospel of, 103
Mauer, Marc, 35
McCain, John, 49, 50, 68
McCarthy, Joseph, 20
McChesney, Robert, 98
McCurry, Mike, 64

McGrath, Marcus, 53
McGuire, Tim, 66
Mecca, 132
Media Studies Journal, 95
Medicaid, 56
Medina, 132
Mein Kampf (Hitler), 109
Mencken, H. L., 159
Mennonites, 106
Meridian (Ill.) High School, 153
Merrill Lynch, 94
Methodists and Methodism, 100–101, 105, 116
Mexico, 27, 114
Miami Herald, 78
Micah (prophet), 135
Michigan, 162; University of, 85, 89
Middle East, 20, 61, 158; crisis in, 64, 83, 100, 118, 130
Mikva, Rachel, 116
Military Order of the Purple Heart, 166
Milton Eisenhower Foundation, 28
Milwaukee, Wisconsin, 144
Minkley, Mary Beth, 144
Minnesota, 117, 162
Minow, Newton, 85
Mintz, Morton, 69
Missouri, 24, 35, 39, 81, 93, 97; University of, 143
Missouri Synod, 106
Mitchell, George, 75
Mohammed, Wallace, 112
Mondale, Walter, 26
Monterey, Mexico, 114
Montgomery, Alabama, 111
Moore, Mike, 17
Moral Majority, 121
Morocco, 158
Morris, Dick, 6–7
Morrison, Frank, 15
Moyers, Bill, 44, 47
Moynihan, Daniel, 57
Mozambique, 42
MTV, 87
Muhammad, 117, 118, 132
Mulroney, Brian, 1, 9, 75, 93
Murphy, Tom, 83
Murray, John P., 85
Muskie, Edmund, 52
Muslims, 20, 44, 73, 74–75, 100, 111; extremist, 14–15, 127, 128, 132; leaders of, 130, 131; nations of, 10, 115, 128; and the poor, 103, 111, 112; violence against, 100, 129, 132–33. *See also* Islam; Muhammad

Nader, Ralph, 38
Nation (periodical), 74
National Academy of Sciences, 35
National Coalition for the Homeless, 55
National Commission for the Prevention of Youth Violence, 85
National Education Commission on Time and Learning, 139, 144
National Enquirer, 67
National Geographic (magazine), 62
National Institute of Mental Health, 82, 88
National League of Cities, 28
National Literacy Act, 154
National Review (periodical), 47
National Rifle Association, 48, 51
National Security Act of 1947, 13
National Urban League, 28
Native Americans, 39, 40
NBC, 37, 59, 77, 80, 96-97, 176
Nebraska, 134, 168, 172
Ness, Susan, 93
Netherlands, 12, 113, 150
Network, 106
Neuborne, Burt, 49
Nevins, Allan, 164–65
New Jersey, 56, 168
Newsweek (magazine), 63, 73, 103, 151
New York, 27, 31, 89
New York City, 9, 32, 41, 73, 107, 131; and education, 146, 169; meetings in, 79, 113–14. *See also* Columbia University; New York University
New York State Psychiatric Institute, 89
New York Times, 32, 64, 67, 88, 92, 94, 113, 168; columnists for, 19, 91, 176; and international news, 78, 81; and international relations, 17, 156; and religion, 73, 107; reporters for, 4, 22, 69
New York University, 49, 165
Niebuhr, Reinhold, 101

Nigeria, 12, 129
Nightline (television program), 64, 72
Nixon, Richard, 6, 19, 32, 90, 129
Nobel Prize, 2
North Carolina, 143; University of, 84
Northern Ireland, 100
Norway, 12, 113
NPR, 80

Oakland, California, 140
Oakley, Robert, 10
Oklahoma, 52, 53–54
Oregonian (newspaper), 67
Oxford University, 15

Pacific Gas and Electric, 172
Pacific Telephone and Telegraph, 172
Pakistan, 10, 14–15, 131, 132
Palestine and Palestinians, 100, 131, 133
Panama, 53
Parade (magazine), 62
Parks, Michael, 80
Pascal, Blaise, 131
PBS, 60, 72
Peace Corps, 162
Pell Grants, 170
Pennsylvania, 73, 107, 133, 168
Pentagon, 44, 73, 157
Peres, Shimon, 61
Peter the Hermit, 133
Pew Charitable Trusts, 107
Philadelphia, 107
Phocion, 7
Plato, 86
Pledge of Allegiance, 110
Plutarch, 7
Portugal, 12
Poundstone, Paula, 46
Powell, Colin, 113
Powell, Michael, 97
Princeton University, 164
Prisons, Federal Bureau of, 29
Producers Guild, 85
Project for Excellence in Journalism, 95
Proposition 13, 171–72
Protestants, 100, 105. *See also names of specific denominations*
Pryor, David, 23
Pulitzer Prize, 94, 165
Putnam, Robert, 5, 72, 135, 162, 173–74

Qur'an, 117, 119

Race to Incarcerate (Mauer), 35
Rand Corporation, 32
Rankin, John, 167
Rather, Dan, 61
Reagan, Ronald, 12, 24, 26
Red Cross, 104
Regular Veterans Association, 166
Rehnquist, William, 33
Reno, Janet, 49
Republic (Plato), 86
Republican Party, 24, 45, 68
Republicans, 23, 56, 57, 169; in Congress, 3, 19, 22, 40, 47, 50, 52–54. *See also names of individuals*
Rhine Valley, 133
Rich, Frank, 176
Roberts, Gene, 92
Robertson, Pat, 112
Rogers, Will, 134
Rome, 77
Roosevelt, Franklin D., 18, 168
Roosevelt, Theodore, 98
Rose, Charlie, 72
Rotary Club, 162
Rowe, Sandra Mims, 67
Rubenstein, Jacob, 112
Rumsfeld, Donald, 20, 44
Russia, 9, 27
Rutgers University, 168
Rwanda, 76, 128–29

Safire, William, 19, 91
Sahara Desert, 158
Salvation Army, 112
San Diego Unified School District, 142
Saperstein, David, 121
Saturday Review (periodical), 165
Saudi Arabia, 128
Sawhill, Isabell, 151–52
Scalia, Antonin, 122
Schlichter, Art, 37–38
Search for Common Ground, 118
Seaton, Edward, 78
Sen, Amarty, 128

Senate, U.S., 30, 53, 70, 114, 120; and campaign contributions, 41–42, 44, 47; committees of, 52, 97, 166; and courage, 16, 58; and education, 162, 164, 167, 171; and the media, 63, 92–93, 94; Republicans in, 3, 52; and taxes, 24; and welfare, 54, 57. *See also names of specific senators*
Sensenbrenner, James, 19
September 11, 2001, attack, 100, 110, 113, 119, 129, 130–31, 156
Seventh Day Adventists, 106, 112
Shanker, Albert, 149
Shapiro, Walter, 6
Shriver, Sargent, x
Sierra Leone, 17
Simon, Martin, 84
Simon, Paul, 8, 32, 101–2, 126–27; campaigns of, 69–70; and education, 154, 172; and foreign aid, 17; and media, 62–63, 92–93; and political contributions, 41, 43; and prisons, 30, 31, 33; and religion, 73, 103, 112, 122
Simon, Sheila, 126
Simpson, Alan, 23
Simpson, O.J., 60
Singapore, 139
Sixty Minutes (television program), 72
Smith, Al, 74
Snyder, Donald, 30
Social Security, 21–24
Social Text (journal), 165
Sokal, Alan, 165
Solarz, Stephen, 158
Somalia, 10–11
South Dakota, 27, 39
Southern Baptist Convention, 118, 122
Southern Baptist Theological Seminary, 109
Southern California Edison, 172
Southern Illinois University, 27, 32, 33, 93, 112
Soviet Union, 3, 16
Spain, 12, 129, 150
Spanish, 156, 158, 160
Springer, Jerry, 96
State Department, U.S., 2, 11, 113, 126, 127–28
Steeleville (Ill.) High School, 153
Stelle, John, 168
Stephens, Don, 39
Stinger, Howard, 83
St. Louis, 39, 93, 97
St. Louis Post-Dispatch, 24, 81
St. Matthew Lutheran Church, 108
St. Olaf College, 162
Sudan, 9, 129
Supreme Court, U.S., 18, 90, 129; justices of, 33, 122
Sweet, Lynn, 65

Talbott, Basil, 65
Talmud, 103
Taylor, Charles, 16
Taylor, Paul, 70
Telecommunications Act of 1996, 92–93, 94–95
Temporary Assistance for Needy Families, 55
Tennessee State University, 143
Texas, 97, 118, 146, 151; University of, 84
Thailand, 162
Thatcher, Margaret, 24
Third Reich, 87
Thompson, James, 57
Thompson, Tommy, 56
Thurow, Lester, 170
Time (magazine), 73, 87
Times (London), 6
Times-Mirror Corporation, 95
Time Warner, 98
Tobacco Institute, 82
Topping, Seymour, 81
Torah, 119
Truman, Harry S., 2–3, 5
Tunis, 100
Turkey, 24
Turner, Ted, 83, 98
20/20 (television program), 72
Tyndall Report (periodical), 80

Uganda, 77–78
Unitarians, 74
Unitarian Universalists, 112
United Jewish Federation, 106
United Kingdom, 150
United Nations, 10, 47–48, 76, 126, 127;

and the poor, 110, 112, 114; secretary-general of, 13, 17; and the United States, 51–52, 156
University of California, 37, 84, 89, 91
University of Chicago, 83, 96, 108, 122, 132, 149, 154, 159
University of Idaho, 162
University of Illinois, 27, 37, 98, 126
University of Maryland, 115
University of Michigan, 85, 89
University of Missouri, 143
University of North Carolina, 84
University of Notre Dame, 13
University of Texas, 84
University of Wisconsin, 84, 168
Urban II, 132
USA Today, 144
U.S. News and World Report (magazine), 37, 75
Utley, Garrick, 80

Vandalia State Prison, 30
Vandenberg, Arthur, 3
Vermont, 58
Veterans of Foreign Wars, 166
Vietnam, 11, 126; war in, 159, 162
Vines, Jerry, 118
Virginia, 19, 84
Voter News Service, 65

Wall, James, 75
Wall Street, 72
Wall Street Journal, 50, 64, 70, 78
Washington (state), 86, 118–19
Washington, D.C., 39, 73, 75, 121, 126, 167; media in, 65, 75; and political contributions, 46, 48–49
Washington, George, 4, 24, 39, 71, 122
Washington Monthly (periodical), 69
Washington Post, 19, 43, 64, 69, 70, 78, 131
Watson, Jerome, 65
Webster, Daniel, 41
Weekly Standard (periodical), 74
Wehmeyer, Peggy, 73
Wellstone, Paul, 54, 57, 93
Wesley, Charles, 100–101, 111
Wesley, John, 100–101, 111
West Virginia, 56
Wheaton College, x
White House, 10–11, 49–50, 76
white people, 127
Williams, Brian, 72
Williams, Patricia, 74
Wisconsin, 56, 144–45; University of, 84, 168
Works Progress Administration, 54–55
World Economic Forum, 79, 113
World Health Organization, 48
World News Tonight (television program), 80
World Trade Center, 73, 100, 157
World Trade Organization, 17, 45
World Vision, 106
World War I, 159, 167
World War II, 53, 91, 134, 166, 168, 170
World Wrestling Federation, 87
Wyden, Ron, 97
Wynn, Steve, 40
Wyoming, 134

Yale University, 159
Yugoslavia, former, 129

Zinni, Anthony, 10

Paul Simon serves as the founding director of the Public Policy Institute at Southern Illinois University Carbondale, where he also teaches courses in political science, journalism, and history. Prior to joining the faculty in 1997, he was the senior U.S. senator from Illinois. He has served on the budget, labor and human resources, foreign policy, judiciary, and Indian affairs committees. He is the author or coauthor of nineteen books, including *Freedom's Champion: Elijah Lovejoy*; *Tapped Out: The Coming World Crisis in Water and What We Can Do about It*; and *PS: The Autobiography of Paul Simon*.